Community Matters

Also from TERRA NOSTRA PRESS

*Common Ground: International Perspectives
on the Community Land Trust*

*En Terreno Común: Perspectivas Internacionales
sobre los Fedeicomisos Comunitarios de Tierras*

Community Matters

Conversations with Reflective Practitioners
about the Value & Variety of Resident Engagement
in Community Land Trusts

Edited by John Emmeus Davis

TERRA NOSTRA PRESS
Madison, Wisconsin, USA

TERRA NOSTRA PRESS

Center for Community Land Trust Innovation
3146 Buena Vista Street
Madison, Wisconsin, USA 53704
https://cltweb.org

Illustrations: Bonnie Acker
Book design: Sara DeHaan

Publisher's Cataloging-in-Publication Data:
Names: Davis, John Emmeus, editor.
Title: community matters : conversations with reflective practitioners about the value and variety of resident engagement in community land trusts. / John Emmeus Davis, editor
Description: Madison, WI: Terra Nostra Press, 2022.
Identifiers: Library of Congress Control Number: 2022913287 | Paperback ISBN: 979-8-9861776-0-1 | ebook ISBN: 979-8-9861776-1-8
Subjects: LCSH Land trusts. | Land tenure. | Land use. | Land use, Urban. | Nature conservation. | Landscape protection. | Sustainable development. | Economic development—Environmental aspects. | City planning—Environmental aspects. | Community development. | Urban ecology (Sociology) | BISAC POLITICAL SCIENCE / Public Policy / City Planning & Urban Development | LAW / Housing & Urban Development | BUSINESS & ECONOMICS / Development / Sustainable Development | SOCIAL SCIENCE / Sociology / Urban
Classification: LCC KF736.L3 W49 2022 | DDC 333.2—dc23

*Dedicated to the memory of
Reverend John Whitfield (1950–2022),
a servant leader and faithful builder
of the beloved community.*

When we talk about community land trusts, there can't be a trust without community organization. People are the core. They can't be an object; they must be a subject. They have to lead the process.

—Alejandro Cotté Morales,
Chapter Two

It's important to ensure that community-led projects are the way forward, rather than us going in to become saviors. Each community is the expert in understanding what their own community needs.

—Razia Khanom,
Chapter One

There's still this desire to bring about an opportunity where we can see the best in each other; where we're able to celebrate achievements, not only locally but throughout the globe; to realize that individuals have a desire in their hearts, minds, and spirits to see the Beloved Community become a reality.

—Rev. John Whitfield,
Chapter One

CONTENTS

Contributors   xv

Featured Organizations   xxiii

Keeping "Community" in Community
Land Trust: Variations on a Theme
John Emmeus Davis   xxvii

Community matters, in more ways than one   *xxx*

Weaving together the strands of engagement   *xl*

Conversations with reflective practitioners   *xlvi*

1. **Building the Beloved Community: A Panel
   Discussion with Geert De Pauw, Razia Khanom,
   Mariolga Juliá Pacheco & Jason Webb**
   Moderated by Theresa Williamson, September 27, 2021   1

   The "beloved community": An opening reflection
   by Reverend John Whitfield   2

   Who is the "community" served by your CLT?   5

   How can CLTs become more inclusive?   10

   Diversifying the leadership of CLTs?   14

   Has the CLT movement fallen short in building the
   beloved community?   17

2. **CLTs and Community Organizing: A Panel Discussion with Ashley Allen, Alejandro Cotté Morales, Geert De Pauw & Tony Hernandez**
Moderated by Dave Smith, December 7, 2021   23

Practitioner stories: getting started as a community organizer and the role of community organizing in creating your CLT   25

Can a CLT be created and sustained *without* community organizing?   45

Do CLT homeowners actually care whether their CLT is community-led?   50

Can an organizer also be a developer?   53

3. **A Conversation with Tony Hernandez & Jason Webb, Dudley Neighbors Inc.**
Hosted by Maria E. Hernandez-Torrales, April 4, 2022   55

Unpacking the meaning of "community"   56

Cataloguing the benefits of resident engagement   60

Dealing with divisions within Dudley   66

Partnering with "outsiders"   70

Overcoming barriers to participation   74

Keeping alive the flame of participation   77

Balancing the roles of organizer and developer   79

4. **A Conversation with Razia Khanom & Dave Smith, London Community Land Trust**
Hosted by Greg Rosenberg, March 30, 2022   85

Organizing continues after a CLT is established   88

Benefits for residents who get involved in the London CLT   90

Putting some fun into community work   93

Giving voice to the "community"   95

Balancing the roles of organizer and developer   99

Resolving conflicts   101

Expanding the CLT's service area   104

New tools for organizing after the pandemic   106

Building trust   109

5. **A Conversation with Geert De Pauw, Brussels Community Land Trust**
Hosted by Dave Smith, April 21, 2022   113

Why is community involvement the "right" thing to do?   115

The place of "community" in *Organismes de Foncier Solidaire*   120

Organizing and building where people are poorer and land is cheaper   122

Dealing with conflict   124

Strategies of organizing and engagement   126

Celebrating success   129

6. **A Conversation with Mariolga Julia Pacheco &
   Alejandro Cotté Morales, Caño Martín Peña
   Community Land Trust**
   Hosted by Line Algoed, February 28, 2022   133

   Governing the land trust and guiding development
   in the special planning district   135

   Benefits of resident engagement   139

   Dealing with diversity   143

   Managing divisions and conflicts   147

   The role of outside professionals in supporting
   community leadership   150

   Strategies for overcoming obstacles and sustaining
   resident engagement   153

7. **A Conversation with Ashley Allen, Houston
   Community Land Trust**
   Hosted by John Emmeus Davis, March 22, 2022   161

   Community organizing versus resident engagement   165

   Organizational benefits of resident engagement   168

   Who is your "community"?   173

   Bridging racial, ethnic, and linguistic divides   176

   Becoming a part of "something bigger than yourself"   178

   Being an organizer versus being a developer   180

   What keeps you going? How do you keep your eyes
   on the prize?   183

8. **Concluding Thoughts: Community Land Trusts**
   As Scaffolding for Continually Thriving Communities
   Theresa Williamson, July 25, 2022   187

   Addressing the gamut of human needs   188

   Trust, engagement and power   189

   From grassroots to meta community-building:
   a virtuous, sustainable cycle   192

   Seven generations thinking   193

Contributors

LINE ALGOED is a PhD Researcher and Teaching Assistant at Cosmopolis, Center for Urban Research at the Vrije Universiteit in Brussels, where she is working on a PhD about collective land tenure as a climate change adaptation strategy. She works closely with the Caño Martín Peña Community Land Trust in Puerto Rico on international exchanges among communities involved in land struggles. She is Vice President of the Center for CLT Innovation, an NGO supporting community land trusts and similar strategies of community-led development on community-owned land. She was a co-editor of *On Common Ground: International Perspectives on the Community Land Trust*. Previously, Line was a World Habitat Awards Program Manager at World Habitat, and a Director at the International Urban Development Association (INTA). She holds an MA in Cultural Anthropology from the University of Leiden and an MA in Sociology from the London School of Economics.

ASHLEY PAIGE ALLEN is Executive Director of the Houston Community Land Trust. Previously, she was a community organizer for over 10 years in Chicago, helping to develop campaigns for improved homeless services, affordable housing policy, and education. Ashley's experience as a homeless youth is what ignited her passion to increase housing accessibility and affordability for people most in need. She serves on the board of The Coalition for the Homeless of Houston/Harris County. She holds a BS in Food Science from Florida A&M University, an MPA from Governors State University, and a PhD in Cultural and Educational Policy from Loyola University Chicago.

ALEJANDRO COTTÉ MORALES holds a PhD in Social Policy from the Graduate School of Social Work of the University of Puerto Rico, Río Piedras Campus, where he is an Adjunct Professor. He has over 25 years of experience as a community social worker. From 1994 to 2002, he directed the Community Development Area of the Península de Cantera Project. In 2002, he became Director of the Citizen Participation and Social Development for ENLACE and the Caño Martín Peña CLT. He was instrumental in guiding grassroots organizing and participation processes around those initiatives, as well as advising on comprehensive development.

JOHN EMMEUS DAVIS is President of the Center for CLT Innovation and Editor-in-Chief of Terra Nostra Press. He is a partner in Burlington Associates in Community Development, a consulting cooperative that has assisted over 120 CLTs throughout the United States since its founding in 1993. He previously served as his city's housing director in Burlington, Vermont under Mayors Bernie Sanders and Peter Clavelle. His publications include *Contested Ground* (1991), *The Affordable City* (1994), *The City-CLT Partner-*

ship (2008), *The Community Land Trust Reader* (2010), *Manuel d'antispéculation immobilière* (2014), and *On Common Ground* (2020). He also co-produced the film, *Arc of Justice*. He holds an MS and PhD from Cornell University.

GEERT DE PAUW has been active for more than 20 years championing the right to housing in Brussels as an activist and community worker. In 2008, following a study visit to the Champlain Housing Trust, he began advocating for the establishment of a CLT in Brussels. He coordinated the CLT feasibility study that was commissioned by the Brussels Capital Region. He has been a coordinator of the Brussles CLT since 2012. He was also a co-founder of SHICC (Sustainable Housing for Inclusive and Cohesive Communities), a European partnership to create a thriving CLT movement in Europe.

TONY HERNANDEZ is the Affordable Housing Technical Assistance Director at Grounded Solutions Network in the United States. He previously served as Director of Dudley Neighbors Inc., a community land trust established by the Dudley Street Neighborhood Initiative in Boston in 1988. DNI has combined community ownership of land, community control of development, and permanent affordability of housing to revitalize a large section of Roxbury that had long been scarred by vacant lots, abandoned buildings, and arson-for-profit. Tony and his family have been CLT homeowners for the past 20 years. He has a Master's degree in architecture.

MARÍA E. HERNÁNDEZ-TORRALES holds an LLM in environmental law from the Vermont Law School and an MA in Business Education from New York University. She studied for her undergraduate and Juris Doctor degrees at the University of Puerto Rico. Since 2005 she has been doing pro bono legal work for the Proyecto EN-LACE and for the *Fideicomiso de la Tierra del Caño Martín Peña*. Since 2008, Hernández-Torrales has worked as an attorney and clinical professor at the University of Puerto Rico School of Law where she teaches the Community Economic Development Clinic.

RAZIA KHANOM is Vice Chair of the London Community Land Trust. She lives in South London with her husband and children, where she has spearheaded the London CLT's efforts to develop Community Land Trust homes at Christchurch Road, an historically diverse area of Brixton. Involved in the CLT's efforts in south London since its inception, Razia is also an active member of the local Muslim community and is involved in young persons' education. She has qualifications in finance and works in a local school.

MARIOLGA JULIÁ PACHECO directs the Office of Community Engagement and Social Development of the Caño Martín Peña ENLACE Project. A graduate of the Beatriz Lasalle Graduate School of Social Work at the University of Puerto Rico, her first approach to the Caño was as a volunteer and later as a student intern. She has served as Special Projects Manager of the *Fideicomiso de la Tierra del Caño Martín Peña*, where she led the process for the granting of surface rights deeds to its members. One of her roles has been the institutional and participatory governance development of this collective land tenure instrument. She is part of the team that put the law and regulations into practice.

GREG ROSENBERG is a co-founder of the Center for CLT Innovation and serves as the Center's Coordinator. He is also a principal of *Rosenberg and Associates*, a consultancy focused on affordable and sustainable housing, cohousing, CLTs, and urban agriculture. He was a founder of the CLT Network and the CLT Academy in the USA and served as the Academy's first director. He previously led the Madison Area CLT, where he developed Troy Gardens, an urban eco-village featuring a working farm, community gardens, a restored prairie, and a 30-unit mixed-income cohousing project. Greg is an attorney and social worker, as well as a LEED Accredited Professional.

DAVE SMITH is a community organizer and affordable housing practitioner. He served for several years as Chair of the London Community Land Trust, the largest CLT in the UK, and was the organization's founding Executive Director from 2008 to 2014. He previously worked for the British Council and on Barack Obama's 2008 primary and presidential campaigns. More recently, he has worked at the National Housing Foundation and is currently Head of Communities at Eastlight Community Homes, a nonprofit housing provider based in Essex and Suffolk. He holds degrees from King's College, the University of Cambridge, and The Bartlett School of Planning, University College London.

JASON WEBB is Community and Technical Assistance Principal at Grounded Solutions Network in the United States. He oversees training and technical assistance for cities, nonprofit organizations, and community groups and assists with the implementation of housing policies and programs with lasting affordability. He previously worked for 15 years at the Dudley Street Neighborhood Initiative and Dudley Neighbors Inc. in Boston, Massachusetts. There, he served in several capacities, including Director of Real Estate and Technology, Director of DNI, and Director of Administration and Finance. He also created a youth development/youth jobs program called *CommunityScapes*. Jason attended Boston University's School of Management.

REV. JOHN WHITFIELD was Director of the Mobile Regional Center for the Alabama Institute for Deaf and Blind and Senior Pastor at the New Zion Church in Fairhope, Alabama at the time of his death in July 2022. He was a graduate of the University of South Alabama. He later served as Executive Director of the Baldwin Housing Alliance, Vice President of the Alabama Association of Community Development Corporations, and Vice President of the Alabama Asset Building Coalition. He was a trainer for NeighborWorks America and a member of the boards of the National CLT Academy, the National CLT Network, and the Center for CLT Innovation. He cofounded Men of Valor and Purpose, a mentoring program for at-risk youth.

THERESA WILLIAMSON, PhD, is a city planner and the founding executive director of Catalytic Communities, an NGO working to support Rio de Janeiro's favelas through asset-based community development. CatComm produces RioOnWatch, an award-winning local-to-global favela news platform, and manages Rio's Sustainable Favela Network and Favela Community Land Trust program. Theresa is an advocate for the recognition of favelas' heritage status and their residents' right to be treated as equal citizens. She received the 2018 American Society of Rio prize for her contributions to the city and the 2012 NAHRO Award for her contributions to the international housing debate.

Featured Organizations

BRUSSELS COMMUNITY LAND TRUST
Brussels, Belgium
2021 *World Habitat Award Winner*
http://www.cltb.be

Community Land Trust Bruxelles (CLTB) was formally incorporated in 2012, after four years of planning and organizing by activists from several housing and neighborhood associations. Although established to serve all of the Brussels Capital Region (population 1,100,000), CLTB has been especially active in the city's poorest neighborhoods like Anderlecht and Molenbeek. The first newly constructed homes developed by CLTB were inhabited in 2015, followed in subsequent years by additional multi-family housing projects being built at various locations across Brussels. CLTB has also played a major role in disseminating the CLT model in other cities in Belgium and in other countries in Europe.

CAÑO MARTÍN PEÑA COMMUNITY LAND TRUST
San Juan, Puerto Rico
2015 *World Habitat Award Winner*
http://cano3punto7.org

The Caño Martín Peña CLT (*Fideicomiso de la Tierra del Caño Martín Peña*) was planned and designed by residents of seven neighborhoods surrounding the Caño Martín Peña, a highly polluted tidal estuary that runs through the center of San Juan, Puerto Rico. The Caño CLT was established in 2004 with the aim of regularizing land ownership and avoiding gentrification and involuntary displacement, an anticipated result of the planned dredging and clean-up of the channel by the U.S. Corps of Engineers. Creation of the Caño CLT and the channel's ecological restoration are among the main elements of the wider ENLACE Caño Martín Peña Project.

DUDLEY NEIGHBORS INC.,
DUDLEY STREET NEIGHBORHOOD INITIATIVE
Boston, Massachusetts USA
https://www.dsni.org

Dudley Neighbors Inc. (DNI) is a community land trust formed in 1988 to serve the Roxbury/ North Dorchester area of Boston, Massachusetts. DNI was an outgrowth of years of grassroots organizing and participatory planning by the Dudley Street Neighborhood Initiative (DSNI). In 1989, DSNI made history by becoming the first and only community-based organization in the United States to win the power of eminent domain. DNI and DSNI remain tightly intertwined today, sharing staff, resources, and a corporate umbrella. More importantly, they share a mission and vision of comprehensive neighborhood revitalization in which community ownership of land and community empowerment of the area's residents go hand-in-hand.

HOUSTON COMMUNITY LAND TRUST
Houston, Texas USA
https://www.houstonclt.org

Nonprofit organizations and community activists, concerned about the rising cost of housing and the threat of gentrification in African-American and Latino neighborhoods in Houston, began considering a CLT as early as 2015. When these areas were heavily damaged by a hurricane in 2017, City officials realized that a CLT might be a critical tool for rebuilding, while also making homeownership more widely available for households of limited means. The Houston CLT was incorporated as an independent nonprofit the following year. Working in partnership with Houston's Housing and Community Development Department, the Houston Land Bank, and other affordable housing organizations, HCLT is grounded in principles of community engagement, equitable access to high-quality housing, and long-term stewardship for permanent affordability.

LONDON COMMUNITY LAND TRUST

London, England

https://www.londonclt.org

Founded in 2007, the London CLT is currently the largest CLT in England. It grew out of a community organizing campaign led by Citizens:UK to create 23 resale-restricted, owner-occupied homes at St Clements, the site of a former National Health Services hospital in London's East End. There are now projects being planned or developed in Lewisham, Southwark, Redbridge and Lambeth, as well as ongoing campaigns in other boroughs. London CLT ensures its homes are genuinely and permanently affordable, as prices on sale and resale are linked to local wages rather than to valuations on the open market.

Keeping "Community" in Community Land Trusts: Variations on a Theme

John Emmeus Davis

Community land trusts proclaim "community" to be their most valued partner in the places they serve, the projects they develop, and the residents they involve in the inner workings of their organizations. They are not alone, of course. The entire field of community development is replete with nonprofit corporations and local cooperatives making similar claims. What distinguishes CLTs from many of their peers, however, is the degree to which an ideological and institutional commitment to community involvement is woven into the culture, structure, and operation of the CLT itself. This participatory element is just as important to what a CLT *is* and *does* as its distinctive approach to the ownership of land and the stewardship of housing.

Ask CLT practitioners—staff members, board members, or outside professionals—what makes their CLT special. They are as likely to talk about their organization's relation to *people* as its relation to *property*. For them, community matters as much as tenure. But they are just as likely to express widely different opinions as to what "community" means, why it matters, and how best to engage residents of the neighborhoods served by a CLT in the organization's affairs.

Multiple conceptions of the meaning and value of "community" go hand-in-hand with multiple forms of resident engagement—strategies that often change as an organization evolves. CLT practitioners are fond of saying that "community organizing never stops." But the process of building a constituency for a CLT when it is getting started is very different than the process of keeping residents vested and involved in the organization over time. Strategies for resident engagement become more varied, too, as a CLT's portfolio of land and housing grows bigger or when its territory expands.

The variety of ways in which "community" is being conceptualized and operationalized in the larger world of CLTs can be seen as a ringing endorsement of the model's adaptability. It is also a testament to the creativity of the movement's leaders. CLT practitioners are continually inventing new ways to give voice to people and places they have pledged to serve.

Not everyone sees it that way. There are any number of researchers, advocates, and critics who view the current state of the CLT movement in a less positive light, warning of a withering commitment to "community" among local CLTs.[1] Variations in resident engagement that depart from what is known in the United States as the "classic" CLT are especially suspect, seen as symptoms of decline rather than as signs of health. As one researcher recently lamented, bemoaning the lukewarm support for resident engagement she discovered among the staff of several CLTs she had studied, "How did a model of community ownership and local democracy become so diluted that 'community' was hardly a part of the process anymore?"[2]

This judgement strikes me as being overly pessimistic, although I confess to having voiced similar concerns on many occasions.[3] Worries about "keeping the 'C' in CLT" are, in fact, not entirely misplaced. There are CLTs that started out with every intention of eventually incorporating the tripartite board and the voting membership of a "classic" CLT, but they have delayed doing so. There are other CLTs that never intended to include these participatory features at all.[4] Still others have dutifully retained the organizational scaffolding for an engaged constituency, but the resources devoted to sustaining this activity have grown less over time, caused by a lack of political will, a lack of staff capacity, or simply the daily grind of getting affordable housing financed and constructed. A high-performing CLT is expected to be a productive housing developer *and* a responsive community organizer, but it is tough wearing two hats. Some CLTs tilt toward the former at the expense of the latter.[5]

These cases notwithstanding, the situation is not nearly as bleak as the picture painted by critics who conclude that community is "hardly a part of the process anymore." My personal observation, having worked with dozens of CLTs inside and outside the United States over the past few decades, is that community *still* matters. Most CLT practitioners, old and new, remain passionately committed to processes of informing, engaging, connecting, and empowering residents of the places they serve and the projects they build. Community has not been lost, nor is it withering away, although the manner in which it is conceived, purposed, and practiced has become increasingly complex.

The practitioners whose conversations were recorded for the present volume epitomize the persistence of this commitment—and its complexity. They were chosen because the CLTs with which they are associated have been especially effective in keeping "community" at the center of their programs and deliberations, putting engagement on a par with development. They were also chosen because, in their personal stories and professional careers, they have shown unwavering support for popular participation in guiding and governing their organizations, while demonstrating a willingness to modify their approach when warranted. They bring both a wealth of experience and a critical eye to this whole endeavor, making them an unusually insightful cohort of "reflective practitioners"[6] for whom the "C" in CLT remains an article of faith, rather than a rigid orthodoxy from which any deviation is forbidden.

Their own organizations have, in fact, sometimes strayed from the straight and narrow path of the "classic" CLT in the composition and selection of their governing boards.[7] Their more significant departure, however, has been to multiply the ways in which people participate. Governance is not the only path their CLTs have followed when endeavoring to involve residents in the work they do and the decisions they make. Other forms of resident engagement are equally important. They represent different strategies for giving "community" a voice in their organizations—different ways for making "community matter."

Community matters, in more ways than one

Few words are more familiar in everyday conversation than "community"—and few are used less precisely. Even in scholarly journals, where a high degree of precision would presumably be a requirement, the term has proven surprisingly slippery. A researcher once reviewed dozens of articles in social science journals where "community" had figured prominently. He found 94 different meanings.[8] Another scholar, looking back at that research, noted that "community" is the rare concept that never carries a negative connotation. People may not agree on what "community" means, but it always refers to something unquestionably good, something desirable.

What is true in the abstract realm of academia is also true in the practical realm of community development. Practitioners employed in the challenging business of developing affordable housing, revitalizing disinvested neighborhoods, or delivering an array of social services to low-income residents use "community" in multiple ways. It sometimes refers to a place. It sometimes refers to the people who inhabit that place. It sometimes refers to the relationships among those inhabitants. These meanings are often used interchangeably, moreover, with little regard for the differences among them.

CLT practitioners carve out a particular niche for themselves within this crowded field. The model of tenure they employ has different features from one country to another and, sometimes, from one city to another within the same country. A generic description that would fit a majority of CLTs, however, is that of a nonprofit, nongovernmental organization promoting *community-led development on community-owned land of residential buildings and other land-based assets that remain permanently affordable.*

The linchpin of this definition is "community," of course, although it must be said that CLT practitioners use the term as loosely as everybody else. One must listen closely to the context to know whether they are talking about the geographically defined area in which their nonprofit organization has chosen to concentrate its activities or whether they are talking about the people who reside there—or some subset of that population.

Dig a little deeper, however, and it becomes clear that what CLT practitioners usually mean by "community" is neither geography nor residency, but the inter-personal **connections** that arise within a place of residence among people who live in proximity to one another. Neighbors interact. They become familiar. They sometimes become friends. They act individually, on occasion, to care for a neighbor in distress. They act collectively, on occasion, to improve the neighborhood or to defend it against a perceived threat. These relationships, these connections, are what distinguishes a community from a territory.

Places of residence provide especially fertile seedbeds from which the tendrils of community emerge. These connections of sentiment and solidarity grow naturally, organically within residential neighborhoods of every type—urban, suburban, and rural. But CLT practitioners do not leave these connections to chance. They intervene to nurture their growth within the territory their CLT has prioritized for the acquisition of land, the development of housing, and the long-term stewardship of permanently affordable homes.

That is not to belittle inter-personal connections that happen within the place of residence *without* the nurturing touch of a CLT practitioner. All of these relationships have value, one way or another. All are part of the web of inclusion and care to which most CLT practitioners aspire in hoping to create, through their organization's holdings and their own efforts, a "beloved community." But some connections have a more immediate, utilitarian value in furthering the mission of the CLT; some are essential to the CLT's success. These are the tendrils that CLT practitioners selectively and intentionally strive to cultivate.

Many different meanings and manifestations of "community" are to be found in the conversations recorded in the coming chapters, including a number of times when the speaker is clearly referring to a particular geography or the population residing there. More often, however, "community" refers to one of five different types of inter-personal connections that result from the skilled intervention of talented CLT practitioners: **solidarity, constituency, mutuality, consultancy,** or **reciprocity.** These are my terms, by the way, not those of the reflective practitioners who are featured here. They use different words when discussing what "community" means and the various forms that engagement can take in connecting residents to each other—and connecting them to a local CLT.

I should point out, too, that community and property are seldom far apart in a CLT, whatever the form of resident engagement. When CLT practitioners lend their hands to knitting people together, it usually has a specific purpose related to parcels of land a CLT is trying to acquire, to units of housing a CLT is trying to build, or to the stewardship of lands and homes entrusted into a CLT's care. Property is the public stage on which solidarity, constituency, mutuality, consultancy, and reciprocity take turns dancing in the spotlight.

Separately and together, these strategies enable those who live on and around the organization's holdings to become active participants in a CLT's programming, rather than passive recipients of a CLT's largess.[9]

Solidarity matters

Community has meaning as "solidarity" when connections are nurtured among residents, organizations, and enterprises throughout the CLT's service area for the purpose of creating a common vision for the development of that territory and building collective power to make that vision a reality. These connections are inherently *political* in nature because they are used primarily by CLT practitioners and their allies to influence public policy and to extract resources—land, capital, and regulatory concessions—from governmental entities in support of the CLT.

The experience of the London CLT is illustrative, but many other CLTs have had similar experiences. As Dave Smith has said, describing the process of developing the London CLT's first project: "Certainly, in the case of St Clements, it wouldn't have happened without our politics forcing the political will. It was only because we were knocking on the door of City Hall that it eventually happened."

Collective power in the place of residence can also force governmental entities to pay more attention to lower-income neighborhoods that normally receive less investment in public infrastructure and public safety. As Tony Hernandez says, "It makes a difference having a voice and an advocate that can elevate our neighborhood in the eyes of government to assure we're being served" (Chapter Three).

Solidarity has a defensive purpose too, protecting lower-income people against the disruptions and depredations caused by what Alejandro Cotté Morales has called "a capitalist system that is constantly prowling, literally, and affecting the more vulnerable people, the communities living in poverty" (Chapter Six). When a CLT owns land in the heart of such an area, it becomes a bulwark against displacement. To quote Alejandro once again, describing the effect of the CLT's holdings in the neighborhoods along the Martín Peña Canal: "People now have more power. People went from being an object to being a subject.... It's not easy to push someone out if everyone owns the land together" (Chapter Two).

The process of prying resources away from governmental entities or fending off speculative predators is sometimes adversarial. People are organized and mobilized to force concessions from reluctant authorities. At other times and in other places, the process is one of partnering with government. As Jason Webb has noted, talking about the Dudley Street Neighborhood Initiative in Boston,

> "We never did the sort of classic Saul Alinsky organizing, where there always needed to be a boogyman; there always needed to be a target. Our organizing principle came from a more participatory and common-vision standpoint" (Chapter Three).[10]

Constituency matters

Community has meaning as "constituency" when residents of the area served by a CLT are actively recruited into the corporate membership of the CLT and formally granted, through the corporation's bylaws, the right to participate in the CLT's governance.[11] The composition of a CLT's membership and governing board can vary greatly from one CLT to another. In the "classic" model, however, two-thirds of the seats on the board of directors are elected by this constituency. Members are drawn from individuals who occupy homes on lands owned by the CLT or who use the CLT's lands for non-residential purposes. Members are also drawn from people living throughout the CLT's wider service area who are not direct beneficiaries of the CLT's holdings, "people who put themselves forward, who self-nominate and want to be involved," as Dave Smith has described members of the London CLT (Chapter Four).

These connections are *organizational* in nature, bestowing rights and responsibilities on a legally constituted membership and giving that constituency a degree of control over the organization that is charged with owning land, doing development, and performing stewardship on behalf of the residents of a particular place. Some CLTs turn the participatory thermostat way down, giving members minimal say in the CLT's affairs, even to the point where, as happens in the French version of the CLT, some CLTs do not have a membership at all. At the other extreme, there are CLTs like the Caño Martín Peña CLT in Puerto Rico which turn the thermostat way up. There, as Mariolga Juliá Pacheco relates, the organization's leaders and staff believe:

> People must be part of the governance structure of every CLT at all times; not only at board meetings, but every day. Because this also produces a sense of ownership towards that common space that we want to protect, and we want it to be a successful space for everyone involved (Chapter One).

When it comes to cultivating a constituency, resident engagement can be a complicated affair. CLT practitioners must concentrate simultaneously on increasing the *number* of organizational members, strengthening the *vertical* connections between the CLT and its members, and encouraging *horizontal* connections among the members themselves. Many CLTs hold property across a wide territory, moreover, serving multiple neighborhoods. This can create special challenges, as Geert De Pauw has said about his own CLT in Belgium, where members are spread throughout the Brussels region:

We tried to create a community out of them, trying to connect people and to organize some community activities with them. We wanted to get more people involved in the life of the community land trust and give them a sense of belonging to some wider community. . . . There were some positive results out of it. But we didn't really manage to create a movement where everyone who wanted a home and became a member of the CLT would feel a part of it (Chapter Five).

Mutuality matters

Community has meaning as "mutuality" when connections are nurtured in the place of residence that are primarily *social* in nature. These are informal, inter-personal relationships that enable neighbors to interact respectfully and familiarly, enjoying each other's company, celebrating special occasions, and lending a hand when needed. As Razia Khanom says, "That's what we do in communities. We help each other, we support each other, and we're also inspiring each other" (Chapter Four).

While neighborly relations of sentiment and care can grow naturally among people sharing the same geography, CLT practitioners have a particular interest in seeing them flourish in the residential projects they develop and manage, especially in multi-unit cooperatives, condominiums, and rentals. The CLT in Brussels is a case in point. After falling short in their initial efforts to instill a "sense of belonging" among members spread across the capital region, CLTB narrowed its focus and adjusted its strategy. In the words of Geert De Pauw:

Now, as more and more housing projects are getting developed, we are investing more time and energy in building local communities *within* the housing projects—and possibly with the communities living around them—rather than trying to invest in a regional movement with all the people (Chapter Five).

The energies of CLTB's staff are currently being poured into organizing events that help residents to become acquainted with their neighbors and providing trainings that give residents the tools to make collective decisions and to participate in managing their multi-unit projects.

A more expansive notion of mutuality, where bonds of familiarity and sociability extend beyond specific projects, often guides the efforts of CLT practitioners who are focused on revitalizing an entire neighborhood—or, in the case of the Caño Martín Peña CLT, improving a cluster of neighborhoods. This is what Mariolga Juliá Pacheco means, I believe, when she talks about interpersonal relationships improving a homeowner's "quality of life in the spaces outside the four walls of one's home" (Chapter Six), or when Dave Smith talks about the London CLT being in the business of building "continually thriving communities" in addition to building homes (Chapter Four). Tony Hernandez eloquently describes this more extensive notion of mutuality when he says:

> The model looks to preserve this old-school feel of a village, a place where your children can play outside and your neighbors are watching over them when you cannot. The essence of that lies in weaving all of these pieces together. Whether you have a market-rate home or a community land trust home, the goal is that we ultimately share those resources and those benefits, so at the end of the day we can live successful lives with our families. I would like to think that's the main goal of a CLT (Chapter Three).

Consultancy matters

Community has meaning as "consultancy" when a CLT has a culture and a policy of constantly reaching out to residents of the neighborhood(s) it serves in order to hear their concerns, to solicit their advice, and to accept their guidance in planning the organization's projects and programs. These connections are primarily *informational* in nature. Their purpose is not power (solidarity), governance (constituency), sociability (mutuality), or stewardship (reciprocity), but communication. When a CLT makes consultancy a key part of its planning and programming, the CLT is transparent in sharing information, intentional in soliciting it, and responsive when receiving it.

This process of listening and responding to residents of the place(s) served by a CLT often begins in the early days of planning the organization. It continues, for most CLTs, long after the organization is established. Tony Hernandez likens the latter to the CLT serving as a "doctor" who is regularly "taking the pulse of the community; having a diagnostic of what's really going on" (Chapter Three).

Consultancy can also happen on a case-by-case basis whenever a new land use or a new project is proposed. For some CLTs, "community-led development" is less about governing the organization that is sponsoring development and more about the process of informing and involving proximate stakeholders every time a development is planned. For example, it was a standard practice of the Brussels CLT in their first residential projects to get prospective homebuyers involved in helping to design the housing they were eventually going to occupy. At the London CLT, there is a policy of actively engaging residents of each neighborhood in which a new project is to be developed.[12] At the Caño Martín Peña CLT, there is an organizational "climate," according to Mariolga Juliá Pacheco, that presumes the inclusion of "affected parties in decisionmaking processes" (Chapter Six). Those who are "affected" by a proposed project may or may not be members of the CLT, but because they live in proximity to the site, they are consulted and heard. Mariolga goes on to explain:

> We include the people who are closest to a particular situation
> and give them the opportunity to have a say, participating in the
> decisionmaking and other tasks related to what is going to happen

in that space. This goes beyond a board. Even when the board includes members of the land trust and representation from the larger community, there will always be a more local level of what's happening in those spaces.

Reciprocity matters

Community has meaning as "reciprocity" when the relationship between a CLT and the people who are using its lands and inhabiting its homes is one of shared responsibility, where both parties are equally vested in making this marriage of convenience function smoothly, amicably, and openly over the course of many years. It is a relationship that originates in connections that are essentially *contractual* in nature, but that matures in many CLTs into a stewardship regime that is more *collaborative* in operation and effect.[13]

The CLT, in these cases, does not merely impose conditions and enforce restrictions on the use and resale of property. It cultivates a trusting, supportive relationship with the people who make use of the CLT's lands and who inhabit its homes, an inter-personal connection that continues long after development is done. As Ashley Allen explains:

> We have a stewardship responsibility. We're not just building housing and washing our hands. We have a different perspective than a traditional builder. We have a different perspective than maybe a municipality who's building affordable housing and selling it and then good luck trying to find somebody at local government to respond if there are any problems (Chapter Seven).

This expansive perspective on a CLT's stewardship responsibilities is shared by many CLT practitioners. As one of Ashley Allen's peers said several years ago, describing her own CLT in Albuquerque, "We are the developer that doesn't go away."[14] For CLTs like these, the enforcement of affordability controls (and other provisions in the ground lease) remains a priority. But stewardship also includes the preservation of buildings, making sure they are soundly constructed and well-maintained. Stewardship also includes protection of the occupants' security of tenure, preventing predatory lending and making sure that people do not lose their homes if they get behind in paying their mortgages or utilities.[15] More fundamentally, the responsibility of CLTs that have a reciprocal relationship with their leaseholders is to stand behind them, in good times and bad, helping them to succeed in the housing that is theirs. As Mariolga Juliá Pacheco says, when describing the relationship between her own organization and the people who reside on the lands owned by the Caño Martín Peña CLT, "They know they have our backing" (Chapter Six).

Admittedly, it is something of a stretch to call a two-party relationship between a CLT and a leaseholder a "community." As a CLT's portfolio grows bigger, however, and as the CLT becomes responsible for an increasing number of leaseholds, more and more threads of obligation and concern crisscross a CLT's service area. It seems reasonable to call that dense network of responsibility and reciprocity a kind of "community."

Weaving together the strands of engagement

Despite elucidating five different meanings and manifestations of "community," I am now going to muddy the waters by admitting that they are not as separate and distinct as I have made them seem. The boundaries between them are quite permeable, one form of resident engagement frequently merging with another.

This happens, first of all, because "the needs of communities are fluid," as Razia Khanom has noted (Chapter One). CLT practitioners are constantly adjusting their priorities to meet those needs, while modifying their approach to involving residents in the delivery of projects and services. That is what Alejandro Cotté Morales means, I believe, when he says that organizing "must renovate itself constantly, responding to people's reality" (Chapter Six).

Resident engagement can also flow from one form to another because, as Geert De Pauw points out, "the political climate can change" (Chapter Five). The clearest example is the back-and-forth between solidarity and other forms of engagement. CLT practitioners may have assumed that the sort of organizing they did in a CLT's early days to build solidarity among residents and allies to attract the support of governmental authorities was no longer needed; they had won the day. But, as CLTs in both Brussels and Houston later discovered, what is given by government can be taken away government. When there is a change in policy or personnel in a governmental agency, CLT practitioners who may have shifted resources toward becoming better stewards of the housing they've created can suddenly discover they must return to a more adversarial, political strategy in order to protect or restore gains they had thought were secure.

Practitioners change strategies, on other occasions, because they learn from their mistakes; or, at least, they realize that what they have been doing is not working as well as they had hoped. They then devise and pursue an alternative strategy that might work better. That's what reflective practitioners do. When the Brussels CLT saw that building a region-wide constituency was not accomplishing what they had intended, for example, they re-allocated resources to focus on mutuality instead. They did not completely abandon their commitment to cultivating a voting constituency, but they dedicated more resources to facilitating connections among residents inside their multi-unit housing projects.

Not only is there fluidity between strategies, there is also a *synergy* among them. CLT practitioners pursue multiple, complementary strategies at the same time. When a CLT does a good job of stewardship, for example, it is deepening the pool of people who can be called upon if organizing for collective power becomes necessary.

As Ashley Allen says, happy homeowners are "major organizing assets . . . our best advocates" (Chapter Two). Similarly, there is an overlap between building a voting constituency and building solidarity, captured nicely in the formula voiced by Razia Khanom: "The more membership we have, the more power we will wield" (Chapter One).

There is also a sense, in listening to these CLT practitioners, of multiple strategies of resident engagement overlapping and coalescing to build connections that radiate far beyond the CLT's own holdings. Even an activity as tightly focused as stewardship (reciprocity) can foster relations of solidarity and mutuality that benefit everyone who resides within a CLT's service area, not just the people who use the CLT's land or who inhabit the CLT's homes. Dudley Neighbors has been especially effective in this regard. In the words of Jason Webb:

> As a CLT, you really have to take community as far and wide as
> possible and be inclusive of everybody . . . That's why, at least
> for Dudley, we did a lot of work in making sure that, as we did a
> lot of stewardship for our homeowners, at specific times we also
> allowed for that stewardship to flow to their neighbors. If we were
> bringing in a contractor, let's say a fencing contractor, and some
> of the neighbors also wanted their fencing done, we didn't say, "Oh
> no, these fencing contractors can only work for our homeowners."
> We would share that information and allow for those other
> homeowners to share in some of benefits we were bringing in.
> (Chapter Three).

One final observation I would make about these multiple meanings of "community" and these multiple forms of resident engagement: a hierarchy does not exist among them. One is not more important than another to a CLT's success; one is not more essential than the others to making community "matter" in a CLT's work. Alejandro Cotté Morales is especially clear on that point:

> We must also be respecting and understanding the different types
> of participation. We have been led to believe that participation
> necessarily implies people attending meetings or assemblies.
> Since we started here, however, we have seen different types of
> participation and they are all equally valuable (Chapter Six).

This is where critics of the CLT's "withering" commitment to community often get it wrong. They concentrate solely on governance—what I have characterized as "constituency"—overlooking the other ways that participation can occur in a CLT. I have sometimes made the same mistake myself.

I have come to accept, however, that participation can assume multiple forms—with varying degrees of internal intensity. There may not be a hierarchy *among* solidarity, constituency, mutuality, consultancy, and reciprocity, in other words, but there is a hierarchy *within* each one. There are different levels of participation, which vary according to the extent to which a CLT's projects, programs, and plans are actually determined by the collective voice of a place-based community. This has been described by the authors of a recent essay, drawing on an earlier academic article, as a "ladder of participation," one that ranges from tokenism at the bottom to community control at the top.[16] The authors apply this imagery to the governance of a CLT, but I would contend that constituency is not alone in this. Every form of resident engagement has its own "ladder of participation." Or, to repeat the analogy I suggested in my earlier discussion of solidarity, each form of resident engagement has an internal thermostat. CLT practitioners, at different times and in different places, dial the temperature of participation up or down, responding to conditions, politics, and needs that are constantly in flux.

This raises a rather thorny issue for practitioners and researchers. What degree of participation is "enough" in judging whether or not community actually "matters" in the organization and operation of a particular CLT? If there are, indeed, five different strategies that CLT practitioners can employ in engaging residents and building community, must all five be present before we can say with confidence that the "C" in CLT is alive and well? What if one or two are missing, but the others are dialed up to the highest degree of participation?

When governance is the only form of participation that is deemed to "matter," critics of the current state of the CLT movement are quick to render a judgement that essentially says, "no constituency, no community." That has essentially been the verdict of those who perceive the commitment to community to be in serious decline. Jason Webb went so far as to say, during the panel discussion recorded in Chapter One, that organizations which lack a voting membership and a tripartite board should not even be *called* community land trusts; in his opinion, they are "frauds."

The problem I find with this particular point of view, despite its sincerity in extolling the virtues of CLTs that are "community-led," is that it places constituency at the pinnacle of a dubious hierarchy, diminishing the value of other forms of resident engagement. It inadvertently praises CLTs that have structured the governance of their organizations along lines of the "classic" CLT, but may have turned the participatory temperature way down on building power within their service areas, building community within their projects, consulting with affected residents before they develop a project, or creating a stewardship regime that goes beyond contractual compliance. Conversely, it denigrates CLTs that have turned the temperature of solidarity, mutuality, constancy, and reciprocity way up, but may possess neither a voting membership nor an elected board. I cannot bring myself to call the former legitimate and the latter fraudulent.

This question of how many kinds and degrees of participation might be "enough" raises the related question of *when* participation should occur in planning and operating a CLT. Alejandro Cotté Morales, for one, is quite clear:

It should be there from the beginning. When we talk about participatory planning, we mean that people should be involved starting from the design phase of their process. Participation makes people feel useful and relevant to the process. Thus, they take responsibility for what happens. If the process is from the top down, if it's implemented incorrectly for lack of active participation, it will not meet the needs of the people; it will not reflect the community's reality (Chapter Two).

But what of CLTs that get started in other ways? There are community land trusts that have been created as a top-down initiative of a municipal government. There are others that been grafted onto the trunk of another nonprofit, the latter of which may have a governing board that is structured quite differently than that of the "classic" CLT. There are also newer CLTs like the one in Houston that have not yet added a voting membership or a stewardship program, waiting until there is a critical mass of homeowners who can get involved in both. In the meantime, the Houston CLT has made resident engagement a high priority, despite lacking a corporate constituency and a robust stewardship regime. They have done intensive engagement to develop what Ashley Allen calls, "a group that supports you and sees your vision and wants to work toward a similar vision" (Chapter Seven).

What has been especially helpful in cultivating these connections, in the case of the Houston CLT, is that the organization's leadership is racially and linguistically representative of the people residing in the places where the CLT has chosen to work. Ashley Allen again:

When it comes to our board, yes, all of it is Black or Hispanic. I do think that's important. . . . I think it helps to have people who understand those communities and their unique perspectives and unique needs, having that relationship and building that trust. I think we benefit from having leadership of color. It's made it a lot easier for us to go into a neighborhood (Chapter Seven).

I resist saying that an organization which has made such a concerted effort to engage with the people it serves—and to look like the people it serves—doesn't deserve to be called a CLT. I believe, in fact, that the Houston CLT is not only a land trust but a *community* land trust, despite lacking (for now) some of the organizational and operational features found in many other CLTs in the United States.

This drives home the point made earlier by Alejandro Cotté Morales. We should respect that there are many types of participation. We should also understand, as Jason Webb has said, that "this idea of community is not always a bed of roses. Some of this stuff is really, really messy" (Chapter Three). That is certainly true—and not necessarily bad. What we learn from listening to the reflective practitioners who are featured in the chapters that follow is that an organization can be deeply committed to keeping the "C" in CLT and can be heavily engaged in giving residents a voice in the organization's affairs even if it employs unorthodox strategies and structures to make that happen. Such variety makes for a messier picture. But, as the title of an earlier essay published by Terra Nostra Press put it, "messy is good."[17]

Conversations with reflective practitioners

The meanings and manifestations of "community" that matter the most to a CLT do not happen by themselves. They are a conscious product of strategic interventions by trained professionals and committed volunteers, a point colorfully made Alejandro Cotté Morales:

Communities can be idealized. "Look, how cute; the community is organized." Well, it's not like that. That did not happen by the grace of the Holy Spirit. It happened because of community organizers.

> People talk about "organic processes," but there's always someone driving things, facilitating things (Chapter Six).

All of the practitioners featured here have been "facilitating things" in their own CLTs for a number of years. On occasion, they have played the role of a traditional community organizer, fostering the sort of group formation and collective action that extracts essential resources from the powers-that-be. As external conditions have changed, however, and as their organization's internal holdings of land and housing have grown larger and more diverse, these practitioners have been called upon to play other roles and to pursue other strategies for incorporating "community" into the fabric of their CLTs.

They have built a corporate constituency for guiding the CLT's decision-making. They have nurtured connections of sociability among residents and neighbors of the housing developed by their CLT. They have consulted residents living near proposed projects, regardless of whether they are members of the CLT, involving them in decisions of design, development, and use. They have endeavored to create a stewardship regime that goes beyond the contractual, cultivating a more collaborative relationship with people who are leasing the CLT's lands and inhabiting its homes.

There is a storehouse of knowledge in the depth and diversity of their experience. When CLT practitioners like these are encouraged to talk candidly and reflectively about the communities they serve, the strategies they employ, and what's worked well (and less well) in fostering greater participation, they teach a virtual master class on the purpose and practice of resident engagement. What can be learned from them is both practical and inspirational. Talking about his own experience in organizing the London CLT, Dave Smith has said, "You've got to tell stories to people . . . which they themselves can then tell to other people. These are stories they can take on, they can own, and interpret and tell to others" (Chapter Two). Practitioner stories are similar. Hearing what motivates practitioners who are striving to keep the "C" in CLT, despite the obstacles put in their path, provides a narrative of commitment and perseverance that can inspire others to keep the faith, to make it their own, and to pass it on.

A forum for mining these experiences and sharing these stories was provided by the Center for CLT Innovation at the end of 2021.[18] Eight seasoned practitioners, representing five different CLTs, were invited to take part in two panel discussions devoted to the place of "community" in the international CLT movement. The first was entitled "Building the Beloved Community." Moderated by Theresa Williamson from Brazil, it was aired as a live stream with simultaneous translation into English, Spanish, French, and Portuguese. The second was entitled "CLTs and Community Organizing." Moderated by Dave Smith from England, it too was aired as a live stream, with simultaneous translation into English and Spanish.

Listening to these discussions on the day they occurred and reviewing the transcripts later on, my colleagues and I at the Center for CLT Innovation realized that some remarkable content had been generated that deserved a wider audience. We also understood that, as informative and inspiring as these panel discussions had been, they had merely scratched the surface. Each of our panelists had much more to say on topics of vital importance to the global CLT movement.

Early in 2022, therefore, we arranged a series of follow-up interviews to delve more deeply into points the panelists had made the previous year. In a couple of cases, these were one-on-one interviews. In three other cases, a pair of people were interviewed at the same time, one from the first panel and one from the second. All of these conversations were recorded, transcribed, and edited for clarity and length.

There was not an interview protocol containing specific questions that were asked of everyone. The individuals who conducted these interviews are reflective practitioners in their own right, with years of experience working with CLTs. They were encouraged to host an informal exchange, following the conversational thread wherever it might lead.

There were several subjects that we urged every conversation to touch upon, however. First of all, we wanted these practitioners to discuss *who* their "community" might be. We encouraged them to talk specifically about the constituencies and beneficiaries of their CLTs. We also hoped they would talk candidly about tensions that occasionally arise among the populations they serve, recognizing that interests and opinions that differ (and sometimes conflict) are a fact of life within nearly all residential neighborhoods.

We wanted them to discuss *how* they have met the twin challenges of recruiting residents to take part in their CLT's work and retaining them over time. Or, as María E. Hernández-Torrales asks in Chapter Three, "How do you keep the flame of participation alive?" We encouraged them to talk candidly, in particular, about strategies for engaging and building trust with people who have been racially and ethnically marginalized. "There's a lot of trauma there that needs to be overcome," as Razia Khanom says in Chapter One.

Equally important, we wanted these practitioners to say *why* they believe participation adds value for the people and places served by the CLT—and for the CLT itself. There are costs incurred by the organization in nurturing connections of solidarity, constituency, mutuality, consultancy, and reciprocity. What are the net benefits that make resident engagement eminently worthwhile?

The answers provided by these reflective practitioners give us a glimpse into the many ways that community still matters in their own CLTs—and for the CLT movement as a whole. They offer a birds-eye view of a participatory landscape more varied and vital than commonly perceived by CLT critics who find few footprints on the ground showing "community" to be alive and well.

To be fair, these tell-tale signs are easy to miss. The model's other components are much more conspicuous. *Land*—acquiring it; developing it; using it—is the foundation for everything a CLT hopes to achieve. *Trust*, stewarding lands and homes entrusted into its care, is the foundation for everything a CLT hopes to preserve. Both the "L" in CLT and the "T" are essential to what a CLT is and does. It makes sense that so much attention is lavished upon them, resulting in a steady stream of technical manuals, policy reports, and scholarly research depicting the many ways that land can be utilized and that stewardship can be done.

Far less attention is devoted to the "C" in CLT, even though this component is just as essential to a CLT's identity and function. Few publications have previously considered why a community's participation in a CLT's activities adds value. Even fewer have attempted to chart the multiple ways in which participation is being facilitated by CLT practitioners throughout the world. On those rare occasions when "community" does catch the eye of advocates and researchers, they tend to focus exclusively on whether residents are represented on a CLT's governing board. Other forms of participation are overlooked or undervalued.

The present publication is a small step toward correcting such longstanding neglect. It is not a detailed roadmap, however, depicting the best route to follow in reaching a desired destination. It is an evocative travelogue, narrated by experienced guides who say why the journey is worth taking and what to see and do along the way.

Its point of departure is a sentiment shared by most CLT practitioners, namely that community matters as much as tenure in the work they do. After that, things get messy. Practitioners ascribe different meanings to "community." They pursue different strategies for giving residents a voice in their organizations. Itineraries diverge.

That is hardly surprising at a time when CLTs are busily diversifying their holdings of land and housing, expanding their territory, and entering new neighborhoods, cities, and countries. When circumstances change, so must the practice of participation—which is precisely what those practitioners have done who are featured in the following pages. Many roads lead to the promised land of keeping "community" in community land trusts.

Notes

1. See, for example, James DeFilippis, Brian Stromberg, and Olivia R. Williams, "W(h)ither the Community in Community Land Trusts?" *Journal of Urban Affairs* 40 (6): 755-769 (2018). Although this article makes the same mistake I have sometimes made, focusing too narrowly on governance, it is a fine piece of constructive criticism, describing how some CLTs are falling short in meeting their own standards and promises of community involvement.

2. Olivia R. Williams, "Community Land Without Grants and Debt: Funding Ecovillage Neighborhoods with Community Shareholders." *Communities*, #182 (Spring 2019).

3. See, for instance, the concluding paragraphs of "Origins and Evolution of the Community Land Trust in the United States," Chapter One in J.E. Davis (ed.), *The Community Land Trust Reader*, Cambridge MA: Lincoln Institute of Land Policy (2010), as well as "Better Together: The Transformative Complexity of Community, Land, and Trust," Chapter Twenty-six in J.E. Davis, Line Algoed, and Maria Hernandez-Torrales (eds.), *On Common Ground: International Perspectives on the Community Land Trust*, Madison WI: Terra Nostra Press (2020).

4. There are a number of CLTs in the USA and in other countries that do not have a membership. A perfect example would be the French version of the community land trust, *Organismes de Foncier Solidaire*.

5. An argument that such a trade-off is neither inevitable nor necessary is provided in *Impactful Development and Community Empowerment: Balancing the Dual Goals of a Global CLT Movement*, J.E. Davis, L. Algoed, and M.E. Hernandez-Torrales (eds.), Madison, WI: Terra Nostra Press (2020). See, in particular, the opening essay by Tony Pickett and Emily Thaden, "Combining Scale and Community Control to Advance Mixed-income Neighborhoods."

6. Donald Schon, *The Reflective Practitioner: How Professionals Think in Action*. London: Routlege (1992). Schon draws on John Dewey's *Experience and Education* (1938) to argue that "reflective practitioners" do not rely on formulas learned in graduate school, but on improvisation learned by what works—and what doesn't—in daily practice. He paints a portrait of professionals who critically reflect upon their practice and make nimble adjustments as needed.

7. A more detailed description of the "classic" CLT can be found in Chapter One of *On Common Ground, op. cit.*

8. George A. Hillery, "Definitions of Community: Areas of Agreement." *Rural Sociology*, 20, 111-123 (1955).

9. This echoes the distinction drawn by Anna Hope, where she talks about the difference between housing development that is community-*focused* and housing development that is community-*led*. To the extent that the "C" in CLT is active rather than passive, a CLT obviously belongs in the latter category. Anna Hope, "Community-led Housing in England: From Adversity to Diversity." *Planning Theory & Practice* 23 (2022).

10. There is a division of labor between the Dudley Street Neighborhood Initiative, which does participatory planning and community organizing, and Dudley Neighbors Inc., which holds land and performs the duties of stewardship. DSNI takes the lead in facilitating solidarity throughout the neighborhood, although DNI is both a partner and a beneficiary. The London CLT and the Caño Martín Peña CLT, unlike DNI, are not subsidiaries of another nonprofit corporation, but like DNI they are beneficiaries

of the solidarity work done by other organizations of which they are a member: Citizens:UK, in the case of the London CLT; and the Group of the Eight Communities (G-8) in the case of the Caño CLT.

11. Rights of membership in the "classic" CLT also include approving amendments to the CLT's bylaws, approving the sale of land, and dissolving the corporation.

12. As Dave Smith says in Chapter Four, "We could probably knock our houses up cheaper and quicker if we didn't involve people in the process. Everything has got a cost-benefit to it. We put huge weight on the participation, the quality of it."

13. In courses taught by the National CLT Academy in the USA between 2006 and 2012, stewardship was described as a "marriage of convenience," where both parties are equally committed to keeping friction at a minimum and to making the marriage work. In such an arrangement, the operational goal for a CLT is to ensure that *compliance is routine and enforcement is unnecessary*. A more detailed description of this collaborative conception of stewardship can be found in J.E. Davis, "Common Ground: Community-owned Land as a Platform for Equitable and Sustainable Development." *University of San Francisco Law Journal* 51 (2017). [Reprinted as Chapter Three in *On Common Ground, op. cit.*]

14. This characterization of a CLT was coined by Connie Chavez, former Executive Director of the Sawmill Community Land Trust in Albuquerque, New Mexico (USA).

15. A dozen years ago, I dubbed the preservation of affordability, the promotion of good repair, and the protection of security of tenure the "three faces of stewardship." Within these three operational goals, there are multiple duties that are performed best as a collaborative effort of the CLT and its leaseholders. The earliest attempt to identify these goals and duties appeared in J.E. Davis, "Homes That Last: The Case for Counter-Cyclical Stewardship," *Shelterforce*, Winter 2008. [Reprinted as Chapter Forty-six in *The Community Land Trust Reader, op. cit.*]

16. Jeffrey S. Lowe, Natalie Prochasca, and Dennis Keating, "Bringing Permanent Affordable Housing and Community Control to Scale: The Potential of Community Land Trust and Land Bank Collaboration," *Cities* 126 (2022). They adapted and applied Sherry Arnstein's "ladder" to community control in a CLT. (Sherry R. Arnstein, "A Ladder of Citizen Participation," *Journal of the American Institute of Planners* 35(4): 216-224, 1969.)

17. Steven Hill, Catherine Harrington, and Tom Archer, "Messy is Good: Origins and Evolution of the CLT Movement in England." Chapter 8 in *On Common Ground, op. cit.*

18. These panels, offered as part of the 2021 International CLT Festival, were co-sponsored by the Center for CLT Innovation and by a consortium of European CLTs known as "Sustainable Housing for Inclusive and Cohesive Cities" (SHICC).

1.

Building the Beloved Community

*A Panel Discussion with Geert De Pauw, Razia Khanom,
Mariolga Juliá Pacheco & Jason Webb
Moderated by Theresa Williamson
September 27, 2021*

THERESA WILLIAMSON: Welcome to a live panel discussion of the efforts being made by community land trusts to make themselves more inclusive. We'll be exploring examples of CLT practitioners who are working to create and to support "beloved communities" around the world.

I'm Theresa Williamson, Executive Director of Catalytic Communities in Brazil, and a board member of the Center for CLT Innovation. I'll be today's host and moderator.

You'll be hearing about the work being done by each of our panelists and CLT practitioners in a moment. Before you hear from us, however, we wanted to open with a meditation from the Reverend John Whitfield, one of my fellow board members at the Center for CLT Innovation. He previously served on the board of the National

CLT Academy in the United States. We've asked him to reflect on the meaning and origins of the "beloved community."

The "beloved community": an opening reflection
by Reverend John Whitfield

Greetings from LA. That stands for "Lower Alabama."

The "beloved community" is a term that first was coined in the early days of the 20th Century by the philosopher and theologian, Josiah Ross. He saw in the midst of the times in which he was living that there was a tremendous need for us to begin to look beyond our individualities, to look at how we could bring ourselves together into spiritual unity.

It was a tremendous time when there was a shift in the dynamics of how individuals began to reflect on who they were, as related to their spirituality. There were major shifts throughout the world, where human beings began to look at themselves beyond their individual space. They began to realize that there is a greater realm of reality in which we are all connected with the divine spirit that allows us to know that we are not many, but one.

In the second half of the 20th Century, Dr. Martin Luther King reinvigorated this idea of the "beloved community." In December 1956, at a Montgomery Improvement Association meeting in Montgomery, Alabama, Dr. King claimed that boycotts and protest marches did not, in themselves, represent the goal of the Civil Rights struggle.

In that particular session, he went on to explain what the goal of the struggle was. Many had believed that the struggle was simply to break down the barriers that prevented human beings from realizing that we are one blood. Many believed it was time to put away the things that had been bringing about fear and discord, not only in the South, but throughout the nation and the world.

Dr. King stated in his speech that the end of what they were trying to do in the beloved community was reconciliation; the end is redemption; the end is creation of the beloved community. It is this type of spirit and this type of love that can transform oppressors into friends.

The type of love stressed here is not Eros or a sort of romantic love or philia, the sort of reciprocal love between personal friends. It is Agape, which is an understanding of goodwill for all people. It is an overflowing love, which seeks nothing in return. It is the love of God working in the lives of men. This is the love that may well be the salvation of our civilization.

Dr. King realized that it was going to be up to individuals who begin to really understand their connectivity and to move beyond the idea that each man is an island. He realized that reconciliation, bringing everyone back into a spirit of harmony, may very well be the salvation of our civilization.

Dr. King's beloved community was a global vision in which all people were sharing the wealth of the earth. In Dr. King's beloved community, poverty, hunger, and homelessness would not be tolerated, because the international standards of human decency would not allow it. In Dr. King's beloved community, racism and all forms of discrimination, bigotry, and prejudice will be replaced by an all-inclusive spirit of sisterhood and brotherhood. Very prophetic.

The very fact that we're here today, gathered together in this session, lets me know and feel within my heart that there's still this desire to bring about an opportunity where we can see the best in each other; where we're able to celebrate achievements, not only locally but throughout the globe; to realize that individuals have a desire in their hearts, minds, and spirits to see the beloved community become a reality.

I submit to you this morning that the CLT movement of the 21st Century and beyond must strive to take the beloved community to the next level and work towards creating and maintaining "Be-love Communities."

And what do I mean by Be-love Communities? Communities that will be created in the future should be ones that are founded on the principles of love; founded on the belief that we are our brother's keeper; founded on the belief that each one of us has a role in ensuring the wellbeing and safety of others.

The Be-love Communities that I envision will catapult us into a time when each CLT would not only simply represent bricks and mortar, would not only represent families coming together, but would be a catalyst that will move this world toward a place of realizing that we must crucially come together in the spirit of unity.

In my tradition, the word of God as recorded in the gospel tells us "Little children, believers, dear ones, let us not love merely in theory with words or with tongue, giving lip service to compassion, but love in action and in truth, in practice and sincerity, because practical acts of love are more than words." Practical acts of love are more than words.

I submit to you that, if we are going to truly make this vision and this movement be what God has created and desires it to be, we must move towards practical acts of love that are more than words. It can no longer be an academic or a theoretical exercise, because the lives of families, the lives of individuals and communities are at stake. Practical acts of love have to be more than words. They have to emanate out of our hearts, minds, and spirit and with every inch of our being.

As we move together, innovation is a good part of the overall understanding of what we're about. We're not going to rely only on things of the past; we're going to be innovative. We're going to bring the CLT movement to a new level where it creates Be-love Communities, communities where individuals know without a shadow of a doubt that what they're doing is not simply a matter of providing housing with affordability in perpetuity. We're creating an atmosphere of love.

I'll close with the lyrics from a very popular song from 1965. The words are simple, but timely and profound. "What the world needs now is love, sweet love. It's the only thing there's just too little of. What the world needs now is love, sweet love, not just for some, but for everyone." Going forward, let the CLTs that we seek to create become Be-love Communities—not just for some, but for everyone.

My time is up. I thank you for yours. Namaste. Shalom. Peace and blessings.

THERESA WILLIAMSON: Thank you very much, Reverend Whitfield. That was a beautiful, beautiful start to our event. You have set a wonderful tone.

Who is the "community" served by your CLT?

THERESA WILLIAMSON: With these powerful words from the Reverend, I'm going to invite our panelists to reflect on his statements and to consider the question of "Who is your community?" Who is the community that your CLT serves? And what meaning does "building the beloved community" have for you and your organization? Is your conception similar to what we just heard from the Reverend John Whitfield—or is it somewhat different?

I'm going to invite, first, Razia Khanom to take the mic and to share with us some reflections from the London CLT.

RAZIA KHANOM: Thank you, Theresa. And thank you, Reverend, for such inspiring words. You remind me of a saying within Islam which states, "A believer can never truly sleep at night knowing that his neighbors are also not satiated." And these themes you will find across all faith groups, spiritual groups, people who are connected to the community.

I'm really pleased that, in this day and age, we still have that connection to our community. That is certainly a starting foundation. We have an understanding of the trials and tribulations of those who came before us and what they went through. It is a crying shame that we're still having to fight the good fight. But it's also a comfort knowing that in this room alone there are people willing to still fight that fight. So I am filled with hope in that sense.

But our communities are no longer just our local communities. We now benefit from having a global community. Events such as this serve to inspire and help us to keep on. As I've explained to one of my colleagues, I see this as a relay race. You carry your baton for as long as you're due to run and then you pass it on to somebody else after taking it. And this is how you create this chain of events.

The needs of communities are fluid, depending on where you are and the challenges that you are facing. But each and every one of us, whether you are a young child, a baby in arms, or someone who's served their community for decades, we all have physical needs: food, water, and shelter being some of the most fundamental. Without these, we can't grow, we can't function, we can't mature, physically, mentally, emotionally. They are universal needs.

And I'm quite proud to see London CLT actually deliver on meeting some of these needs. It wasn't until this panel was being formed that I realized just how in tune the London CLT is with some of the communities we look to serve.

We have a development in East London—a neighborhood which saw riots in 1976—a development led by an amazing women's group because they understood the need to have stable homes. We are currently looking to bring projects to South London. In the 1980s, riots occurred there. And underpinning all our work is that we are seeing homelessness, deprivation, and a resurgence of inequity.

I think we are carrying the baton right now. I think the CLT model, for me, brought back hope that I had lost about a decade ago. It is a sustainable model for us to use going forward. But along the journey we are going to face a number of challenges. We need to be bringing our community with us—and growing our international community and national community—to ensure that we continue to give each other the strength and resolve to continue going forward.

THERESA WILLIAMSON: Thank you, Razia. Now we'll hear from Jason Webb.

JASON WEBB: Thank you, Theresa. And thank you Reverend John. Great to see you. I remember our days together in the National CLT Academy.

So, the beloved community... I can speak from the perspective of my own community back in Boston, Massachusetts in the neighborhoods of Roxbury and Dorchester where I grew up. I truly saw, and I continue to see, what Reverend John talked about.

In my community, growing up, about half of the land was vacant and abandoned. It was the result of white flight in the 1970s and 1980s. And we faced a lot of arson-for-profit. When property owners did not have any hope to get their investment back on their property, they would literally burn their buildings down. Sometimes the buildings would be vacant. Sometimes there would be families in there. What I grew up seeing was a lot of burnt-out buildings. Then the City would come along and just demolish them.

It took the community coming together and realizing that, "Wait a minute, we are more powerful together than we are as individuals. We're gonna push back and we're gonna start taking back our own community." And that's what they did, through organizing, through planning, through some political maneuvers to get some municipal power to actually start their community land trust.

Now, the Dudley Street Neighborhood Initiative is getting close to about 40 years old. They've done amazing work. I remember growing up and being a part of community meetings where there was simultaneous translation because we wanted to make sure that, if we were going to succeed, if we were going to move forward, we all needed to feel like we're on the same playing field. That's what the simple idea of translation can bring you; you don't have to be ashamed that you don't understand English. That has been a barrier for too many communities.

Reflecting on the Reverend John's words, I can say that growing up, when the community was in need, the community really came together. When there were small spikes of violence, you would see neighbors come out and console each other. When there were beefs, we would work on reconciling it ourselves and not allowing others to do it.

I feel like growing up, you know, I was a part of a beloved community. I see it from afar now. It's what drives my work every day as I work with other communities, as they think about using the CLT as a tool that can actually help to spawn a beloved community.

THERESA WILLIAMSON: Thank you, Jason. Now we're going to hear from Mariolga Juliá Pacheco from the *Fideicomiso* in San Juan, Puerto Rico.

MARIOLGA JULIÁ PACHECO: Hello everyone. I work with the Caño Martín Peña Community Land Trust. Our land trust is based on the United States model, but it is subject to the Spanish Civil Code, which governs our legal framework. Our land trust is one of the first documented experiences of applying the model in informal settlements. I'm grateful for the invitation to join this panel and delighted about the conversation we are about to have.

First of all, I would like to thank the Reverend for such inspiring and inclusive words. I believe inclusivity should be one of the main items on our agenda. The land trust movement must provide an inclusive opportunity for all kinds of families and people who occupy different spaces. From the standpoint of that conceptualization, we should really promote solidarity among ourselves, among community groups, and among groups with different interests, finding common threads in the diversity of our communities.

In the case of the Caño Martín Peña, we are talking about a diverse community where solidarity, a history of community action and, above all, our collective memory has kept us together for over 18 years. Hopefully, through the land trust and through G-8, an organization that brings together the leadership of the eight informal settlements along the Martín Peña Canal, we will be able to have a strong community that will be standing for many, many years in defense of the rights of its residents. We also want to ensure that these residents will be able to live out their full citizenship in San Juan, the capital city of Puerto Rico.

THERESA WILLIAMSON: Thank you so much, Mariolga. Now, Geert De Pauw from the Brussels CLT.

GEERT DE PAUW: We started in Brussels some 10 years ago with our community land trust. Our main goal was to tackle the housing crisis that was emerging in Brussels. And we wanted to serve those people who were the hardest hit by this crisis: the poorest families in Brussels, people who had to leave the city, or had to live in bad conditions.

So from the very beginning, we looked for ways of including those families. Brussels is one of the most diverse cities in the world. And this diversity is also very much represented in our community. Today, we have five projects in which some hundred families live there. And we have some 600 or 700 families who are applying to become homeowners.

Most of these people have their roots outside of Belgium. Many of them are refugees or recent migrants, having been born in 66 different countries in Africa, Asia, and all parts of the world. As we only do multifamily developments, people with very different backgrounds live together in our housing projects; also, most of our projects are developed in the poorest neighborhoods of Brussels, neighborhoods where there is often quite a lot of tension.

The great diversity of our residents and the fact that many of them have stressful lives because of their low incomes, this puts quite a bit of pressure on these new communities that are created within our housing projects. That is why we think it is important that we support these groups and help them to develop all kinds of initiatives to strengthen the community and to make their lives easier.

We also think there is a lot of potential to do more than just housing, to help people to develop inclusive projects, projects that have a positive impact in the communities where they are situated. We believe that we have a role to play, therefore, that goes beyond just delivering permanently affordable housing.

How can CLTs become more inclusive?

THERESA WILLIAMSON: Now, let's go a little further. Would each of you speak to some of the practical actions your organizations are doing to make CLTs more inclusive and diverse, especially in who is served. Mariolga, could you start this round?

MARIOLGA JULIÁ PACHECO: Of course, my pleasure. For a bit of context, I should point out that there are eight neighborhoods along the *Caño Martín Peña*, comprising a diverse population of close to 24,000 residents. The migrant population within the eight neighborhoods is around 22%. These communities have one of the highest labor participation rates in all of Puerto Rico, if not the highest. Nevertheless, we are one of the poorest and most marginalized areas. A lot of our people work in the informal sector or are self-employed.

From our perspective, experience, and practice, the methodologies we use to work with people are key. If our methodologies are not participatory, we can't expect participatory results; we can't expect people to get involved in decision-making or to actively exercise their citizenship.

In our case, we frequently use popular education as the groundwork for most of our decision-making processes. We begin by acknowledging the historical, social, and political backgrounds of the people that make up our communities. Once we understand the base, we can begin to weave together those common threads that I mentioned before. Weaving together those threads develops the sense of ownership that Jason and Razia described so well. It's our responsibility, along with the communities, to acknowledge that sense of ownership, to highlight it, to be proud of it, and to build on our common threads so that we can keep promoting collective work.

I will share some examples of the work we are doing. We have different working committees within the land trust and within its leadership for the diverse thematic or programmatic areas we work with. We make sure that all sectors from the various neighborhoods are represented in those working committees in terms of the different topics.

We are very proud to say that over 61% of the community leadership at the Caño Martín Peña is women, and that approximately 25% is made up of residents from the migrant population.

Processes of internal leadership training are important. People must be part of the governance structure of every CLT at all times; not only at board meetings, but every day. Because this also produces a sense of ownership towards that common space that we want to protect, and we want it to be a successful space for everyone involved.

THERESA WILLIAMSON: Thank you Mariolga. Jason, could you speak about the practical ways that Grounded Solutions, or the Dudley Street Neighborhood Initiative, or other CLTs you've worked with have tried to make themselves more inclusive and diverse?

JASON WEBB: A lot of the foundation of my work comes from how I grew up as a young man in my own community, trying to figure out my voice. And it's something that, at the Grounded Solutions Network, we talk a lot about as we talk to groups that want to start up a community land trust.

It is not just about the adults in the room. It can't be, because we know that change is going to take time. When you want to plan, or when you want to propose something, you gotta look at the next generation that's gonna be coming up. So, one of the things that we talk a lot about is where are the youth voices? Where are the senior voices? How can we make sure that we are bringing as much input from residents that are living in a specific area as to how this community land trust should be theirs?

We're just technical experts. We know the nuts and bolts of this model really, really well, but it is gonna be up to those residents that live in that area to really dictate how they want to see their community.

One of the things that Reverend John talked about is love and about being connected. But one of the things that we're very clear about with residents is that it's also about power. It's about making sure that you as a community are not gonna be displaced just because real estate markets are going up and there are people who want to move in and push you out. This model is a way to protect that community.

I just got back last week from Louisville, Kentucky where they're creating their first CLT in the Russell community. And the Russell community is where Breonna Taylor used to live. And another young person was shot while I was there. One of the things that a community member said is, "This is important, this CLT thing, but we also gotta go into healing." So right away, as a technical advisor, I had to say, "Okay, we're gonna pivot and we're gonna work with those residents to get them through their healing."

Again, it has to be: What do the residents want? How can they lead? And that's where you get your diversity. That's where you get cultural diversity along with age diversity, as I like to call it. One of the things that I see from time to time is that groups want to leave out the young folks. And I'm usually there to say, "No, no, no, the young folks are what's gonna take this CLT idea and actually move it to the next level."

THERESA WILLIAMSON: Thank you so much Jason. Let's hear from Geert.

GEERT DE PAUW: Well, for us, if we want to be as inclusive as possible, one important issue is that there are no financial barriers. We try to use a pricing policy that makes it possible for everyone, even the lowest income groups, to buy a home at Community Land Trust Brussels. Something that explains why our communities are so diverse is because our housing is affordable for everyone. Also in the housing market, there is a lot of discrimination toward migrants, so it is those communities whose housing needs are the highest—which motivates them to apply for housing with us.

We also work a lot with community organizations and refugee organizations. More and more it's now word-of-mouth that brings people to us. That's how we reach out to get people to come and live with us.

The challenge, of course, is how can we make it possible for everyone to be involved in what we do? And not just be able to buy a home, but also to become board members, to get involved in the activities, et cetera. That is something we are learning day by day. And we still have a lot to learn. What Jason said about inclusiveness towards young people, for instance, is something we definitely should do more than we do today.

THERESA WILLIAMSON: Thank you Geert. And finally, Razia.

RAZIA KHANOM: I'm feeling increasingly inspired as I'm hearing my fellow panelists. There's quite a lot to unpack here.

I am incredibly proud of how the London CLT have formulated themselves in order to ensure inclusivity and diversity. I'm actually a legacy of their attempts at that. I hadn't even known about the existence of community land trusts until a grassroots door-knocking campaign. Somebody knocked on my door and asked what I thought about affordable housing. That was quite interesting, because it's something I was in need of myself at that present moment.

I got involved with the steering group, and it's been a roller-coaster of a ride. I eventually joined the CLT board. And early in the year, I put myself forward for vice chair as a local representative. The steering group that was formed in my local community was instigated by the Advocacy Academy. It's a youth-led organization that tackles equality and injustice.

So my journey with our CLT in London has been all of these elements coming together. My steering group was initiated by young people, and we are very keen to ensure that youths continue to have an active role in our campaigns.

Our board is hugely diverse across genders and we actively assess how our community-led projects are representative of the communities we are serving. It's active work that we do and we take stock of it regularly. The projects that we have are all community-led. And we're very keen to ensure that those voices remain at the forefront.

It's one of the reasons why I'm here today actually—local voices being catapulted to the forefront of our campaign. I'm incredibly proud of the efforts that we have made and we will continue to make as the needs of our communities change.

Diversifying the leadership of CLTs

THERESA WILLIAMSON: Thank you Razia. Thank you everyone.

Here is the first of two questions you might entertain now: What obstacles have you faced in reaching and recruiting underserved populations? Some of you have already spoken to this a little, but maybe you can talk a bit more about those obstacles, including the challenges of involving immigrants and refugees or those at the bottom of the income pyramid.

And there is also the practical question of what are you doing to diversify the leadership of your CLT and to promote racial equity. And we have an audience question here whether you're doing anything special to welcome and to mentor young people. We can go back and forth between these different questions. I see that Jason has raised his hand. So let's start with you Jason.

JASON WEBB: Yeah, great questions. I'm just trying to figure out which one do I tackle first. So first, how do you engage youth? The easiest way that I've been able to answer that is the fact that you gotta get down to their level.

I remember as a youth member at the Dudley Street Neighborhood Initiative, I got pulled into the organization in a very fundamental way. Youth were coming together to do a simple thing like cleaning up a park that we all played in. The adults were there, and we had food afterwards. Then, during the cleanup and as we were eating, the adults were sharing information. And that information was a little bit interesting. So me and my friends, we said, "Hey, we're gonna keep going to these things." Youth are going to be attracted to things that are cool. So that is my biggest message.

When you think about the diversity of leadership in your organization, you have to be very proactive in saying that there needs to be mentorship. There needs to be support. I remember being supported by a number of mentors in my life growing up that, you know, showed me love and compassion, and also taught me some of the finer skills of public speaking and making sure that my ideas were able to come across.

As you continue to work on diversifying your leadership, I'll slide in the idea of trying to figure out how to create safe spaces. I remember a number of years ago, I was working in Denver, Colorado with a predominantly undocumented Hispanic community. People were basically scared to death to go to public meetings because they were worried they were gonna be picked off and deported. So we came up with different strategies for how to make sure that their voices were heard in an authentic way, while continuing to make sure they were somewhat protected by the larger group.

And some families cannot come out at night because, "Hey, we gotta go and feed our kids." So you can do simple things in holding a community meeting of having childcare there, and having translation services, and having a meal. It's the idea of, "Hey, let's all share a meal together. And let's have a conversation about what we should do next." That can break down a number of barriers. You're basically welcoming folks to be part of that "beloved community."

THERESA WILLIAMSON: Razia, I see your hand is up.

RAZIA KHANOM: This one's a bit of a challenging action point. We can't have this conversation of how we can progress without addressing how we arrived here to begin with, particularly with communities that I grew up in: first-generation migrant communities.

There's quite a large trust-building exercise that needs to be done due to decades of racial subjugation. We're just coming out of a pandemic, a worldwide pandemic, and the statistics of who's losing their jobs—and who isn't—are quite dire. We still have a lot of work to do when it comes to racial equality. In order to engage those communities that we seek to serve, we have to acknowledge that there's a lot of trauma there that needs to be overcome.

Trust is not easily given because of their previous experiences. So I think when we try to move forward, it's really important to understand that trauma and not allow their lack of engagement to frustrate us. Once we understand that, and once we have those trust-building exercises, we will undoubtedly see much more engagement.

I've seen that time and again with organizations. I've experienced that myself. It's really important to have people on the board of the CLT who understand those complexities when we're entering these communities. It's important to ensure that community-led projects are the way forward, rather than us going in to become saviors. Each community is the expert in understanding what their own community needs.

THERESA WILLIAMSON: Thank you so much Razia. Now Mariolga.

MARIOLGA JULIÁ PACHECO: Our work is a continuous process of offering support, empowerment, and training to individuals and groups in order to begin passing the baton and ensuring the generational integration that is needed after 18 years of history. To this end we have also created a professional internship so that we can train our people to join the staff.

For us, working with young people is essential for integration and generational succession. We have the LIJAC group (its Spanish acronym translates to Young Leaders in Action), in which we involve them in a process of training and leadership development at both the individual and collective levels.

With that goal in mind, it's important to break away from the rules that deter the participation of young people. In some of our communities, young people can participate in assembly processes, and they can get elected at 10, 12, or 14 years of age. I mean, we need to start by considering how we can include them, not as mere recipients of information but as agents of history, just like adults.

In this respect, there should be an exclusive space for working directly with young people, a planned working space for them to interact with and to integrate into the adult leadership. An important aspect is the struggle against adult-centrism in both discourse and practice. That's where we play an important role in supporting our communities; we can mediate to relieve tensions that may arise between young people and adults because of their different styles, ways of thinking, and life perspectives. We can be mediators in those relationships, cultivating both the relationships and the work in moving forward. They can be agents of their own history today, not just in the future. They are the present and we need to start from there.

Has the CLT movement fallen short in building the beloved community?

THERESA WILLIAMSON: We're going now to our final round. We're going to talk about whether the CLT movement has fallen short of our aspirational goal of building a beloved community—and, if so, what can we do better.

RAZIA KHANOM: I'm gonna be a bit naughty and say I don't think we've fallen short. To develop CLTs is an incredibly difficult challenge in a society where capital rules and capitalism is king. We are the antithesis of that. You're coming up against developers who would rather use land to line their pockets with exceptional profits. We are a thorn in their side. We have fallen short only in the sense that we've got decades of housing inequity. And society is responsible for that.

I've known about the London CLT for only three or four years. I wish there was something more prevalent, something more obvious with the promotion of CLTs. When I am out campaigning or when I'm speaking to community groups, a lot of people are still unaware that such a model exists.

I would love to see us get the word out that these initiatives exist. I distrusted the model when I first heard about it because I thought, "Genuine affordable housing, I've seen that one too many times. Really, how does that work?"

There is so much greed out there. It's difficult to understand that there truly is a community-led nonprofit organization out there. It's really important to make sure that we market ourselves as just that. Our power lies in our numbers. The more membership we have, the more power we will wield.

Therein lies our challenge in terms of trust-building and ensuring that youth have accessibility. Activism can sometimes be the privilege of those who are a little well-off. When you consider some of the most vulnerable, some of the most deprived communities, they don't have the luxury of giving volunteer time to make things happen. Sometimes they're literally living from paycheck to paycheck. So we have to ensure that, when they are unable to speak for themselves, our engagement and our reflection are a true account of their experience.

THERESA WILLIAMSON: Wonderful. Thank you Razia. Okay Jason, can you talk about this point? Razia talked a little bit about how we've fallen short and what we can do better. I suppose those questions go together. So feel free to answer them as one.

JASON WEBB: I can be critical because I've been doing this for way too long. CLTs, at least here in the United States, might finally be on the cusp of getting some real resources from our federal government. As a result, we are now seeing our model being co-opted by nonprofit housing developers that have professionalized themselves and are now going out and creating their own CLTs. But many do not hit the core foundations that we would consider to be the CLT model. They are very insular. They do not allow for membership. They do not allow for a balanced board.

Unfortunately, we are not calling out those organizations and saying, "What are you doing? Why are you calling yourself a community land trust?" That name, because it runs in my veins, means something very specific to me in terms of having some core values that our founders have said, "Hey, we need this to be an open membership. We need to have a balanced board. We need this to be resident-led and community-led."

That's something that has really saddened me in some of my work. I sometimes come across organizations that have been around for a long time and say they want to partner with CLTs, but then they say, "Being accountable to the community? No, no, no. We know what's best. We're professional housers. We know what's best. We're just gonna create our own CLT."

A lot of times these groups are organized, managed, and led by folks that don't even live in the communities they serve. It's a top-down approach where these organizations come in and say, "Oh, we're gonna do this type of housing without asking the community what type of housing works best for their area."

I think that CLTs that understand our roots, that go by those values, should stand up and call out these frauds. Because I think it undermines the idea of a beloved community.

We as a movement have not been disciplined enough. We want to be inclusive. We want everybody under the tent. But for our own survival, I think we need to call out these frauds and say, "No, you are not a community land trust. You can be something else, but you are not community-led. You are not community-driven."

As a movement, we need to do better in continuing to believe in communities. We need to double down and say that the residents who live there truly know what's best for their community.

For me, that's where I feel like this movement has fallen short. We are not calling out these folks who don't have our same values, who don't believe in the beloved community. We need to start standing up and start pointing them out and saying, "If you don't believe in community, you are not one of us. Sorry."

THERESA WILLIAMSON: Fantastic Jason. Thank you. Mariolga, where are we falling short and what could we do better?

MARIOLGA JULIÁ PACHECO: Well, we know that more can be done and that there is always room for improvement. Having said that, I think that a lot is already being done, as Razia shared with us. One example is this multilingual webinar we are doing, where we are acknowledging that, if we want to add voices to this movement, there must be language equity so we can all understand each other and communicate.

I also believe it's very important in terms of the international CLT movement to not see land trusts as a panacea; to not believe that a CLT is the best solution in all contexts, a godsent solution for all communities. No, there has to be a process of critical consciousness among the people who are going to live out this model, who aspire to leave this model to future generations, a consciousness about why, for what, and with whom.

This has to do with what Jason said earlier about the people we associate with. We must beware of wolves disguised as sheep, which is a popular saying in Puerto Rico.

I believe that it's also important to visualize how to keep the voice of the community alive. It's not enough for them to be members of the board of directors; they should also be part of the practical decisionmaking that leads to the implementation of different land trust projects.

Additionally, I believe it's important for regional and international organizations to serve as stewards. Not centralizing the voice from within a particular race, culture, or country. Instead, these spaces must be equitable for all of us who are participating in them. It's important for international movements to refrain from competing directly [with local CLTs] for funding, not proposing projects that seek the same funding. International organizations can lend support and backing to communities or smaller groups without directly competing for financing sources or potential funding.

Those are areas that need to be worked on so that we can keep growing as a CLT movement going forward.

THERESA WILLIAMSON: Thank you Mariolga. As we near the completion of our panel discussion, we're going to ask Geert to reflect on these matters.

GEERT DE PAUW: Yes. Well, from my European point of view, I think that if we want to tackle inequality, then providing affordable housing is one of the most powerful tools. With a growing housing crisis everywhere—in the major cities in Europe and all over the world—we need more affordable housing, especially lasting affordable housing.

What we can add to that with community land trusts, of course, is this community-led aspect. That is a really powerful tool for these communities. But I'm afraid that policymakers sometimes consider community-led housing as something that is more for middle class groups. That's really a danger that we have to fight. They think you cannot let poor communities take their future in their hands.

We as community land trusts can also play a role in making social housing more community-led; and, the other way around, in making sure that community-led housing is more inclusive. I think those are things that we have to do with this community land trust movement of ours.

THERESA WILLIAMSON: Thank you Geert. I want to conclude our

event by thanking all of our presenters, our translators, and everyone who's joined us for this online session. I hope that you've enjoyed it as much as I have. And thank you to SHICC and the Center for CLT Innovation for bringing us all together today. It's been a really wonderful exchange.

2.

CLTs and Community Organizing

A Panel Discussion with Ashley Allen, Alejandro Cotté Morales,
Gert De Pauw & Tony Hernandez
Moderated by Dave Smith
December 7, 2021

JOHN EMMEUS DAVIS: Hola, and good day to all. I'm John Davis, President of the Center for CLT Innovation. Today's discussion of community organizing in the CLT movement is the final event in a series of presentations and conversations that have been taking place since September as part of the first International CLT Festival. While that Festival is now coming to a close, know that the Center will continue to present panels and webinars of topics of cross-national relevance for community land trusts throughout 2022.

In the meantime, while you are eagerly awaiting the Center's next webinar, I want to remind you that the Center has its own publishing house, Terra Nostra Press. Please take a look at our books and our monographs. Many of the people you'll hear from today authored essays that we have been publishing. They will thank you for your support. We have also built the world's largest online library of free technical and educational materials about CLTs and related forms of community-led development on community-owned land. Pay us a visit at *cltweb.org.*

So, with that bit of shameless self-promotion out of the way, let me introduce Dave Smith, a member of the Center's board of directors and President of the London Community Land Trust. Dave will be doing double-duty today as our moderator and as a panelist, discussing a topic that has long been dear to my heart: the challenge of "keeping the 'C' in CLT."

DAVE SMITH: Thank you John, and thank you everybody. Welcome this afternoon from wherever in the world you are, whether it's good evening, or good afternoon, or good morning. Welcome from London, where it's about five o'clock in the afternoon. It's miserable, it's cold, it's raining, but hopefully we're going warm it up this afternoon with a spicy debate around community organizing and community land trusts.

We've got a fantastic panel. So sit back and enjoy. I'm going to introduce each of our colleagues and ask them to give us their name, their city, their country, and their community land trust. In no particular order, other than the alphabetical order of their surnames, we'll start with Dr. Allen.

ASHLEY ALLEN: Hello everyone, my name is Dr. Ashley Allen, and I reside in Houston, Texas in the United States. I'm the Executive Director of the Houston Community Land Trust.

DAVE SMITH: Thank you ever so much. Dr. Morales, over to you.

ALEJANDRO COTTÉ MORALES: Hello, I'm Alejandro Cotté Morales from El Enjambre in San Juan, Puerto Rico, an LLC that works with communities and organizations.

DAVE SMITH: Thank you ever so much, back to Europe now. Monsieur De Pauw?

GEERT DE PAUW: I'm Geert De Pauw, I work for the Community Land Trust Brussels in Belgium.

DAVE SMITH: And back across the Atlantic to a long-time friend of mine, Mr. Hernandez.

TONY HERNANDEZ: Hi everyone, Tony Hernandez, coming to you from Boston, Massachusetts in the United States. I humbly serve as Managing Director for Dudley Neighbors Incorporated, a community land trust.

Practitioner stories: getting started as a community organizer and the role of community organizing in creating your CLT

DAVE SMITH: Thank you ever so much indeed. Here is the plan for this webinar. I'm going to ask each of our panelists to give a brief, five-to-seven-minute opening reflection. We've asked them to come up with a few pictures and to answer three questions: How did you get started as a community organizer? What type of community organizing went into your community land trust? And what is your main reflection on the role of community organizing within CLTs and the CLT movement?

Once we've had those presentations, I'm going to open up with a few questions that we prepared in advance. And we're very keen to hear from our audience as well and try and get some interesting conversation going. So, Dr. Allen, back to you in Houston. The floor is yours.

Ashley Allen: Houston Community Land Trust

ASHLEY ALLEN: Hello again, everyone. How did I start as a community organizer? Well, the first two pictures that you see at the top of the slide are two shelters for families that are experiencing homelessness. I lived with my family in both of those shelters in Charlotte, North Carolina in the United States. In that moment of experiencing homelessness, I didn't realize that it would be a catalyst for my future work. I guess, as they say, "there's a reason for everything."

My experience with homelessness is what drove me to start trying to change systems to ensure that other families and other young people didn't have the same experience that I had with my family.

In the bottom picture, I have on a yellow shirt. I'm standing in front of a group of organizers and leaders that I worked with at the Chicago Coalition for the Homeless in Chicago, Illinois. That was how I started organizing. I wanted to figure out a way—selfishly, I guess—to come to terms with my ten years, on and off, of being homeless. My way of being able to cope with that experience was to get involved and to make a change. I reached out to the Chicago Coalition for the Homeless, just to volunteer. And one of the ways they said I could volunteer was to tell my story, and then start to work on changing some of the systems and the policies, advocating for people so they wouldn't have those same experiences.

While I learned to organize around the issue of homelessness, I learned basic organizing tools and strategies. I also went into organizing around education and increasing the minimum wage and workforce development. As we all know, housing is one issue, but housing is definitely connected to other social issues that we need to address if we are to improve housing situations for limited-income individuals and families.

The last slide that you see on your screens is what helped me to start really thinking about organizing and really focus more on affordable housing. This picture is of a neighborhood in Charlotte, North Carolina. This is what it looks like now. Those homes are priced at $600,000 and up. I grew up there, when it looked very different. I actually lived in an elevated trailer in this very neighborhood. You wouldn't know it now, but there was dirt where you see bushes. That little pathway was still there, but it wasn't beautifully paved. It was pretty much gravel and broken asphalt. And everywhere you now see a house, there was a trailer.

While I hated living in that trailer, I felt some kind of way about going back to my old neighborhood, seeing what had happened and knowing that, even after all of my hard work and my mom's hard work, creating a better life for ourselves, we could never afford to go back to our old neighborhood. So I really wanted to focus on how do we create affordable housing, and how do we keep an affordable housing inventory in cities that are rapidly experiencing gentrification.

In the creation of the Houston Community Land Trust, the community really did lead those efforts for many years before we were established in 2018. Communities like Third Ward and Independence Heights in Houston are historically African-American neighborhoods. Residents knew that very soon developers would come and start to acquire that land because of its proximity to center city. We've seen this in cities across the world, where people are moving from the suburbs into the center city. They want to have more access to jobs and easy transportation. But what does that mean for those who currently live in those neighborhoods? It means they're being priced out. Communities like Third Ward and Independence Heights had the good sense to know what was going to happen and started to push this idea locally, within their own communities. They really thought about a community-based land trust for these two neighborhoods.

Then the City decided that affordable housing was really important, because Houston, Texas was growing. Many people were coming into the city and moving here. They thought it was affordable. As people came from more expensive cities, the affordability in Houston started to wane. So the city government got behind the idea that the community had been pushing for years. The City decided to help create an independent nonprofit and to be the funder for the Houston Community Land Trust. But let me be clear; the idea definitely started in the community.

When the community land trust was developed in 2018, we didn't stop going to the communities. I came on as the Executive Director, and we went out to get people to understand what a community land trust was. We didn't want to just jump into a neighborhood and say, "We have houses, come trust us."

One thing you know about community organizing is you have to build relationships. In the bottom pictures you see that we had community meetings at the local community center where we started, the neighborhood where we had our first land trust homes. We went to the grocery store because maybe everybody didn't know about the meeting that was happening once a month at the community center and the library. So we decided also to go to where people are. As you can see in the bottom picture, we're at the grocery store signing people up to get more information about the CLT, giving them an opportunity to learn more.

You have to meet people where they are. That was how the organizing started in the community. The City got involved, the land trust got created, and then we went back to the community to make sure they understood what was happening in their community.

My main reflection is that after all this has happened—with City support and community support—organizing doesn't stop.

Some other key reflections are to educate and to advocate. Who are we educating? Who are we advocating to? The community, practitioners, and city government. We are City-funded. So you'll see down at the bottom that we have a picture of going to city council and getting them to understand what we're trying to do in order to have their continued support. They help to fund us, but they also want to know what exactly we are doing. What are the results? Are you coming to the district that I represent?

As you see in the bottom picture to the left, we also had a conference for practitioners and other housing organizations. That's a picture of CLT affordable housing legend Mr. Gus Newport, speaking and telling people about how the CLT movement happened very early on.

Another main reflection is that the homeowners in our homes are major organizing assets. Why? Because people want to see results. People are not going to get behind you if they don't see what you've done. These three pictures are homes that have been purchased through the CLT here in Houston. Our homeowners are essential to us doing well. If they're not happy, if they don't feel like they're supported, they're not going to continue to push the movement forward. They're our best advocates. They are our best representation of the energy and efforts that have been put behind the CLT. They are the people who helped to organize the CLT and can now tell the story. They're the ones who can begin to educate and advocate and let people know what's happening. They help us to craft what our CLT will look like and what the movement looks like moving forward. Pictured here are some of our homes but the people inside the homes are what make the CLT movement continue to grow here in Houston, Texas.

DAVE SMITH: Ashley, thank you so much for your powerful practitioner story. I'm sure it's in no small part responsible for the success of the Houston Community Land Trust so far. I particularly liked it when you said, "We've got to meet people where they are." I think that's so true, meeting them not only geographically in the shops and the barbershops and where they are, but emotionally and politically. We've got to meet people where they are.

I'd like to move on now to Alejandro Cotté Morales. Alejandro has over 25 years of experience in Puerto Rico as a grassroots organizer. He also somehow managed to fit in a PhD in that time and he is an educator as well. I will hand the screen over to him for his story.

Alejandro Cotté Morales: Caño Martín Peña

ALEJANDRO COTTÉ MORALES: Thank you all for this opportunity. Today, I will be talking based on the experience of the Caño Martín Peña in San Juan, Puerto Rico. So, my respects to their leadership.

There are three fundamental areas related to how I began working as a community organize. First, on the photo to the left, you can see the public housing project in San Juan where I was raised. I grew up in poverty and marginalization. As the saying goes: "Necessity is the mother of invention." Within the needs we had, I was allowed and compelled to have freedom of movement, creativity, and collective work in order to survive the everyday idleness and wants that are experienced by those of us who have lived in poverty and marginalization. That required us to create recreational spaces, places where people could speak and engage as a community. And, obviously, the delicious madness presented by el barrio—the neighborhood—engenders a will to survive.

From that oppression and need, you inadvertently start acquiring community organizing tools and skills. For example, the sense of brotherhood, leadership development, sense of humor, creativity, and honesty typically seen in el barrio; the loyalty and sense of justice, the empathy and, above all, something very important in community organizing: the cunning and street smarts, the barrio zest that you need when you work as an organizer.

Another important factor that shaped me was having the opportunity and privilege to attend the University of Puerto Rico to study community-based social work. My graduate studies were in community organizing. So I was able to apply the theory to the practice, the theory from a critical point of view, where human dignity is non-negotiable and social justice is pursued. This gave me the unique opportunity to have a critical view and to apply what I mentioned before: street smarts and theory.

The third important aspect of my training was the chance, besides other community work, to work on two innovative projects in Puerto Rico: the Península de Cantera project and the Caño Martín Peña ENLACE project. For almost 27 years, I was able to learn from the communities there and in other projects where I worked. To learn from them and to work along with the community in their processes, in which they always played the lead role.

So, what type of organization was created as part of the Community Land Trust? Nosotros Primero was an organization created within the Caño Martín Peña Community Land Trust, meaning that the experience is relevant to the El Caño communities in San Juan.

A bit of background can help to understand the context. Puerto Rico is a colony of the United States, so it's a neoliberal capitalist system like many others in the world. In and of itself, this presents a challenge when talking about collective property. Capitalist systems encourage individualism, and here you faced the challenge of working with a collective vision within a community.

El Caño communities comprise 26,000 residents living in an area of San Juan. These are people who came to the city from the country when the economy transitioned from agriculture to manufacturing. They were literally forced to look for jobs, to strive for a better quality of life in Puerto Rico. They occupied lands on the banks of the body of water known as the Caño Martín Peña.

Our people have lived here for over a hundred years. After many years, the area where they are living is near the San Juan financial district. Those lands are very valuable to the private and public sectors. The people were afraid of disappearing as a community, which other sister communities had experienced as a result of gentrification.

This fear of disappearing forced the community leadership to identify alternatives to protect their community. And the opportunity came up to draft a bill, developed and created by the community and aided by lawyers with a sense of community. After the community itself introduced the bill, it was approved by the legislative and executive branches. What did they create? They created a community land trust, which at the time comprised 78 hectares. Currently, the project has grown to include 110 hectares.

The difference between the Caño Martín Peña Land Trust and

many other land trusts is that people already lived there. We are talking about a community that had been there for over 100 years. This created a sense of ownership, an urge to legalize the land where your house sits. People believed they had a right to the land and a right to housing. And that right to the land and to housing helped them organize. And the fear of disappearing as a community encouraged people to put religion and politics aside. There was a need to come together as a community in order to create strength and to have power. When the chance to do so came up, obviously with community organization and a fighting spirit, the people of the Caño Martín Peña created public policy.

People now have more power. More than 150 surface rights deeds have been issued. Imagine now owning together over 110 hectares. So, in that sense, the community is powerful. It's not so easy to push someone out if everyone owns the land.

People went from being an object to being a subject. We are talking about century-old communities who now have the right to be part of their country's development. What are the insights gained by this process? From the community organizing process comes the insight that community organization is the backbone of any CLT. When we talk about community land trusts, there can't be a trust without community organization. People are the core. They can't be an object; they must be a subject. They have to lead the process.

First, the organization creates power and fights off market forces and gentrification. If people do not get organized, it's easier to defeat them one by one. Having to deal with a solid organization that meets frequently and is always mindful of its processes is a totally different thing.

Another takeaway is the importance of comprehensive community development. It can't be seen as one dimensional. In other words, it can't be considered exclusively an urban or spatial physical issue, or as a point of law. It needs to be comprehensive. The people and the community must be involved. The work has to be done from the individual to the collective and vice versa.

The process is complex and we should be mindful of that. Our support needs to be permanent but not tutelary, so as not to create dependence. It should help people understand the progress of the ongoing tasks, but should also consider that everyone has their particular situations.

And, all the while, there is an oppressive and manipulative system, shifting every four years in the case of Puerto Rico and every five or six years in other countries. This system is always looking for ways to retain the land and to undermine the collective. So part of the support to be given by organizers is to constantly open up spaces for critical thinking and community organization.

One last insight is that community land trusts must include community organizing and social work components. We need to have behavioral experts involved in this process. In other words, community land trusts can't be created solely with architects, planners, and lawyers. If there is no behavioral expert working from within the collective, from the process of the perceived needs, then we can't call it a community land trust. In that sense, there is an opportunity to open up spaces for critical thinking among the people. They become empowered. They are the ones who keep the land trust strong.

DAVE SMITH: Very important conceptualization of right space and the discourse there as well. Where you differ from everybody else is that your CLT is about legalizing something which already existed, rather than building it from nothing. That is a really interesting starting point.

ALEJANDRO COTTÉ MORALES: Exactly, we are talking about communities in informal settlements, just like many others around the world. But the great accomplishment here is that these organized communities were able to legitimize their right to the land and now collectively to own more than 200 hectares in the Caño communities.

I seriously doubt that any model that focused solely on the individual would have been able to make it. Community organizing work is crucial because it's what allows the work to advance at the collective level. You know, it's a community land trust. It speaks about collectiveness, about community, not about individuals.

Sadly, systems always turn to individualism, because the easiest thing to do, in a way, is to divide people on the basis of religion, politics, and the economy. These are matters that affect them individually, but these are also matters relevant for the collective; they are matters of collective needs. So it would be impossible to build strong processes regarding a land trust—processes that transcend and evolve without losing sight of their mission—without community organization.

DAVE SMITH: Thank you ever so much. We'll come back to that later on, no doubt. I want to come across the Atlantic now to my European brother Geert De Pauw. (Britain is in Europe, regardless of what anybody else will tell you.) I've known Geert for a long time. I'm incredibly impressed by his grassroots organizing in neighborhoods in Brussels which don't always get the best press. He does a fantastic job of showing you the better, truer side of these neighborhoods. So, Geert, over to you.

Geert De Pauw: Brussels Community Land Trust

GEERT DE PAUW: Thank you Dave. And hi everyone. In this photograph, you can see our community at one of our assemblies. I got involved in community land trusts because I'm trained as a social worker and a community organizer. I worked for many years in a community center in the municipality of Molenbeek, where we worked on housing issues. Due to rising housing prices in Brussels, more and more families couldn't find decent housing, especially large migrant families.

That's why we decided to develop a community-led housing

project together with a social housing provider. The residents would call their project "L'Espoir"—or "Hope." In order to provide the best possible solution, we wanted to closely involve the people with housing needs in this project. We brought together fourteen low-income migrant families to develop this project together with us. The homeowners played an important role in every step of the development process. The success of this project gave us confidence in a community-led approach toward affordable housing.

At the same time, in my spare time as an activist, I was involved in a movement for the right to housing. One of the important actions for us was the occupation of an empty monastery with the Coalition of Squatters Homeless Associations and the Federation of Associations for the Right to Housing. We occupied this huge building that had been empty for years in order to create temporary housing for people in need. It was also a way of putting the housing issue on the political agenda.

During these actions, the first seeds were planted for what would become the community land trust, because some of the later founders of the community land trust of Brussels got to know each other through these actions. There the idea grew that perhaps we should not only demand for the politicians to build affordable housing for the poor; we could also bring together people with housing needs to be part of the solution.

We were inspired by historical examples in Belgium, like the Belgium Workers' Cooperatives. They were responsible for some of the most beautiful social neighborhoods in Belgium. Also, the cooperatives in South America were an inspiration for us. But then we got to know the CLT model and we understood that this was something that corresponded to what we were looking for, so we started to organize for the creation of the CLT in Brussels.

Organizing or setting up a community land trust is not so difficult, but the problem, of course, is getting resources and getting land to build homes. In a city like Brussels you cannot do that without the support of the authorities. So, when we started organizing, a very important target in our organizing strategy were the regional elections of 2009. In the months leading up to the elections, we tried to inform as many people as possible about the CLT model. We brought together a coalition of organizations, but also families in housing need to discuss with them the concept during what we called "people's assemblies." We organized a few of them. You can see by the venues where we organized them, how broad this coalition was. The one picture is taken in the conference room of the Christian Workers Movement. The other photo was taken in the community space of a squatted industrial building.

When the newly elected Minister of Housing announced that he wanted to make room in his policy for innovative housing models, we had a well-founded proposal ready. It was supported by a group of 20 organizations and a few hundred citizens in need of housing. This was really crucial in convincing the regional government to invest in what was then an unknown concept. And to invest in people who had very little experience in building housing.

Our community organizing approach has always been rather constructive, with the most important aim being to show that there is a lot of support for the idea. This worked, because in 2012 we got funded by the government to develop two pilot projects.

Once our CLT was recognized by the region and received subsidies, we re-oriented our community work. In Brussels, people who want to buy one of the homes of the community land trust have to become a member of our association. We are a regional community land trust, so our projects are developed in different neighborhoods. And the people who are applicant homeowners are also scattered over the Brussels region. They belong to different ethnic and cultural communities. So we wanted to create more connections between all these people, among all these members. The idea was to build a strong region-wide community, a real movement.

The community-based development approach that we used led to some very interesting results. For instance, pictured here is a group of women who met through this process. They decided to start every week with a guest table, where they cook for whomever is interested to come. The initial idea to create this strong movement among all our members didn't really work out the way we had planned. But, as more and more of our homes are occupied, we have started to re-imagine our approach to community organizing.

Our community work now mainly consists of strengthening the communities in and around our housing projects. We bring future residents together before they move into their homes. Also, after they have moved in, we support them and help them to set up all kinds of initiatives to strengthen their own community. For instance, bicycle lessons or neighborhood kitchens, or homework support within our housing projects. And when organizing collective trainings and activities, we also try to connect people living in different housing projects.

This new approach is very promising. We hope it will not only lead to resilient communities within our housing projects, but will also become the basis for a real CLT community that we can build upon to defend our organization. Because, while today we have strong political support, things can change rapidly. Community organizing can then become of crucial importance again.

DAVE SMITH: Geert, thank you so much for your presentation. It was great to see those streets again. For people who don't have the misfortune to read the British press, there are some awful right-wing newspapers in the UK, which have described Molenbeek as the heart of Islamic fundamentalism in Europe.

For many of us, the fight for housing justice is inseparable from the fight for racial justice. I wonder what it has been like for you in Molenbeek, where you've been trying to introduce a new concept that describes itself as community-based. Have you ever had the response, "Well, we didn't mean that community. We meant the white community, the European community."

GEERT DE PAUW: I don't think that question has ever been raised. Maybe the opposite. Some of the people who are part of our community ask why there are not more not more white people involved in our community. Our main objective, when we started organizing for the community land trust, was to reach those who are the most in need. In these migrant communities, there's a lot of poverty, but on top of that there's also the factor of discrimination in housing. It is no wonder that most of the people who got interested in our work belonged to these migrant communities.

Brussels is a very, very diverse city, one of the most diverse cities in the world. For example, within CLTB's member community we have more than 68 different nationalities. This gives you an idea of the context we are working in.

DAVE SMITH: We will come back to that question later on, no doubt. Tony Hernandez, I want to come across to Boston and hear from you, if you please.

Tony Hernandez: Dudley Neighbors Inc.

TONY HERNANDEZ: Hey everybody. Thank you for lending your ears to my voice in this webinar and giving me a chance to show off our community land trust here in Boston, Massachusetts in the United States.

One of the questions that was posed to us was how did we start out as organizers? One of the things that I'll disclose to folks on the webinar is that not only am I able to serve as Managing Director for Dudley Neighbors Incorporated; I was also blessed with the opportunity to buy a home on the community land trust in 2001. I found out about this lottery. I found out that I could get homeownership at an affordable price. That was in 2001. I got the opportunity to have my name picked out of the lottery and I managed to buy a home and be a homeowner. Since then, I have been giving of my time to the community land trust board. I served on the board for 13 years, 7 years as its president. I learned about this thing called a community land trust. I've now served as a Director for this community land trust for over 8 years.

I like the mindset as we talk about these things, especially in today's world, when we're dealing with inequality. How do you address equality in today's world? How do you also address equity? Equality and equity are the key words that are being talked about in many circles. But how do we balance them?

Well, one of the things that I think this community land trust model does is aim to strike that balance. It also has an opportunity to introduce justice. As you can see in the picture on the slide, it is not necessarily about building the equality and the equity to reach the fruits on the tree. It's the system that needs fixing. It's not the people; it's the system that needs to be fixed. I wanted to share this slide to kind of frame your mindset in order to not only think about the people, but also about the systems that are impacting the people.

I would imagine that, if you're joining this webinar, you already know what a community land trust is about. Right? But here's the A, B, C definition of a community land trust. It is a nonprofit organization, aiming to develop and to steward housing, community buildings, and commercial spaces on behalf of the community. These become community assets. Our charge is to work on behalf of the community and listen to what the needs of the community are so that we can build physical infrastructure in our neighborhoods that will serve the people who are most in need.

I want to show folks some before-and-after pictures. This is one of our streets here in the Dudley area known as Alexander Street. This is in 1987. Today, Alexander Street looks like this. I want to show the dramatic impact. This is what it looked like before; this is what it looks like today.

And, folks, this is a result of community organizing. My fellow panelists have all touched on it. There's a common denominator here. It's about the community, about the people. What you're seeing in this second picture is a result of people coming together and organizing and having an impact on what the physical revitalization of a neighborhood could look like.

This is another site on our land trust. Notice the yellow tripledecker house in the distance. This is what it looked like around 1987. This is what it looks like today. Notice the same triple-decker yellow house. And this park at the center is owned by the City. But they were cornered into beautifying this park because we managed to build community land trust homes around the perimeter of the park. Because the perimeter was now occupied by community land trust properties, it made sense to turn this into a beautiful park with a sprinkler system there. Just behind this picture, there's a playground. I'm praying that sooner rather than later we can get past all this COVID stuff and can do block parties in this park once again. This is where we get together with the community, throw old-school barbecues, music, people sitting on their front porches, the kids playing, neighbors getting to know each other. That's a lost art. We try to keep that alive in our neighborhood, here in Dudley. We love that we're able to figure out how to inspire some of that through this work that we do with the community land trust.

Next slide, please. These are blocks from back in the 1980s. You drove through this neighborhood and everybody claimed that you were driving through the ghetto. There were illegal trash transfer stations. Folks were burning their houses down to collect on the insurance so they could take off from the neighborhood. It was just a very disinvested neighborhood.

As a result of community organizing and the portfolio of land that DNI has built, we were able to build a number of homes. All of these homes are community land trust properties. The land belongs to DNI, and the properties belong to the homeowners. Part of my job is every day to ask myself, "How can I help our homeowners be the best homeowners they can be?" How do we serve as a resource, and help them take advantage of being in the land trust. How do we educate and empower the people to be able to carry this forward and to help the CLT to grow.

This is a view of what we call the Dudley Triangle. All the colored blocks that you see are blocks that were once empty parcels of land. Over the 35-plus years, DNI has been able to produce 227 affordable units, 97 of them being single-family homes, commercial spaces, community gardens, and playgrounds. At the beginning, we were able to get eminent domain over more than 1300 empty parcels of land as a result of community organizing from the inception of the organization. Today I have only a handful of sites on the land trust that we still need to develop. As a matter of fact, the City is now approaching us to occupy parcels of land outside of this triangular perimeter as a result of the track record that we've been able to produce. To remove land from the speculative market, this is the hustle and the game that we have to play in this community land trust arena, if it's going to be reachable for the less fortunate.

Next slide, please. The community land trust model can also have a huge impact on foreclosures. I had an MIT student come to me. He wanted to do his thesis on our community land trust, but he had no idea what to focus it on. I said, "You know what? I want you to dig up as much information on foreclosures in our neighborhood as far back as you can take it." As you can see here, he was able to get data on the foreclosures within a two-and-a-half-mile radius of our Dudley Triangle from 1993 through 2014.

As you're looking at it, the grayish area represents the catchment area that DSNI, Dudley Street Neighborhood Initiative, serves with its organizing power. The bluish triangular shape in the middle is the 60-plus-acre lot of land that our portfolio exists in. DNI owns more than half of those 60 acres within its land trust portfolio. The MIT student generated this information for me. As you can see here, within a two-and-a half-mile radius of our neighborhood, over a 21-year period, there were 490 foreclosures. Within the larger DSNI target area, that number dwindled down to 365. In our Dudley

Triangle, where the majority of our portfolio exists, only 22 foreclosures happened inside the Triangle.

The magic question, the million-dollar question, was how many of our actual homes were impacted by foreclosure? I really wish I could tell you that we had zero. We had four foreclosures over that 21-year period, but that was because we had a few homeowners that had too much pride and didn't want to accept the help that we were offering to help them save their homes.

That turned into another arm-wrestling match, where we fought with the banks to make sure that these homes remained in our portfolio, and remained affordable. But one other cool fact is that during the foreclosure crisis that the United States was going through, between 2008 and 2012, our community land trust here in Dudley had zero foreclosures. There were zero foreclosures during the foreclosure crisis that we sustained here in the United States.

The impactful statement behind this slide is that over 21 years, across a two-and-a-half-mile radius, land trust properties only accounted for .081% of all the foreclosures during that period of time. The preservation of affordability and the longevity of property ownership, while keeping communities intact, makes a hell of an argument that the power of a community land trust can be real.

Where are we at today? We have produced 97 single-family homes, along with a few duplexes in there, and 130 affordable rental units. We have a 10,000 square-foot greenhouse, multiple urban farms. We bought a former bank building too. There's a lot of development. The common denominator, the most important thing, is that hundreds of families and thousands of community members are being served and put on the path of success because of this model.

DAVE SMITH: Thank you ever so much. Some incredibly powerful statistics there about the ability of your stewardship to defy what's happening elsewhere in the market. And one of the things I want us to come back to later on, when we get into the discussion, is the interesting relationship between the Dudley Street Neighborhood Initiative's community organizing work and the CLT. So, Tony, thank you. Fascinating stuff.

Dave Smith: London Community Land Trust

DAVE SMITH: Ladies and gentlemen, I am going to use the moderator's prerogative of telling you quickly about myself, and the London CLT.

The first thing to know is this picture here. I chose it purely to prove that once upon a time I had some hair. This was taken back in 2008. I was somebody who was always interested in politics growing up, interested in progressive causes. The only politics I knew, because it's the only politics you're taught, is that of party politics, mainstream politics, institutional politics, establishment politics. So I was interested in that.

I volunteered on Barack Obama's primary campaign in 2008, when he was running against Hillary Clinton. This was in Tony Hernandez's neck of the woods in Somerville, Massachusetts. I fully expected to go over there from London and have them say to me, "Here's your green card. We've got you a small office in the West Wing as chief script writer for the President."

That didn't happen, sadly. But what did happen, as I came back home without a job, having failed to impress anybody over there, was that I had learned about Obama's time in Chicago. As a young man, he had worked as a community organizer and been influenced by Saul Alinsky.

When I got back to London, I just Googled community organizing in London. I didn't think we did in the UK, but we did. There was a small group called London Citizens and they had a job opening for one day a week, at minimum wage. It was a housing organizer job. I knew nothing about housing at all. But I think I must have been the only person who applied for the job, because they decided to give it

to me. It was from there, my first job working as a community organizer, that we set up the London Community Land Trust campaign.

What type of organizing went into the creation of the CLT? It grew
out of the work of London Citizens, which was an Alinsky-ish idea of
organizing, engaging with civil civic institutions such as schools and
churches and mosques, trade unions, finding leaders and developing them, and bringing them together.

What we also did, I think rather uniquely, was to tap into a particular sense of place. This is a photograph of Saint Clements Hospital in Mile End, which is in the east end of London, traditionally the
poorest part of London. Saint Clements Hospital was built as a work
house for the poor in 1848. It is now the home of London's first-ever
community land trust. What we managed to do was to engage people in a way where they were able to take a place, which historically
was quite poor and full of bad memories, and turn it into a new vision which they could be excited by and optimistic about.

One of the things we did, led by two wonderful women, Kate Mac-
Tiernan and Lizzy Daish, was to run what was called the Shuffle Film
Festival. We were campaigning to get hold of this particular site for
housing. To engage the local community, to get them to come in and
be a part of our planning, to look at what houses should be built, to
engage them with the CLT, we put on a film festival. A local resident
named Danny Boyle helped us to put it on. This is a photo of people sitting outside watching a big screen, part of the picture that you
can't see. It was a fantastic way of getting people to engage with the
site and to engage with the campaign.

This reflects what Ashley was saying earlier about you've got to
go to where people are. I also think, you can't be culturally exclusive or politically purist about the community organizing work that
you do. I don't care if people are coming to a campaign out of a sense
of what I deem to be the right politics, or if they're coming purely
because they need a house for their family, or if they're coming for

what I believe not to be the right political motivations. You've got to meet people where they are. And where they are culturally as well. You can't be snobby about it. This can't be something exclusively for people who buy into the culture of progressive ideas. I wanted the CLT always just to be the most sensible, worthwhile financial proposition for working families. Putting on the film festival helped us do that.

Finally, I was asked to reflect on the role of community organizing in the CLT movement. I think it's incredibly important. I'd just say the most important part of it is that you've got to tell stories to people. And crucially, you've got to tell stories to people which they themselves can then tell to other people. They can take on, they can own, and interpret and tell to others.

When we started the London Community Land Trust, the first meeting I ever organized had 12 people at it. Now we have got homeowners in South London (very soon), as well as in East London. The membership is in the thousands. Nobody can ever achieve that by trying to organize all those as individuals, by themselves. You have to create stories that people can own and then add their own twist and pass them on.

That's my reflection on the role of organizing in the CLT movement. And a little bit about London and the London CLT, where I come from.

Can a CLT be created and sustained *without* community organizing?

DAVE SMITH: I want to move us now to a discussion of how essential community organizing may be. I'm going to start with Alejandro, if I may, because I think he gave the strongest sense in his presentation that you can't have a community land trust without community organizing. So, Alejandro, do you think it's fair to say that without community organizing, there is no CLT? Or is there a world in which you could have resale formulas, permanently affordable housing, and all the other technical aspects, but no organizing—and still call yourself a CLT?

ALEJANDRO COTTÉ MORALES: Community organization is extremely necessary. But this obviously involves continuous support. I'm not talking about tutelary support; instead, it refers to the kind of support that builds leadership in the communities. With community social work or behavioral experts who fully support people and families in the process of seeing their land trust in different contexts and knowing how times change. Because, obviously, there are people who will begin their own processes, young adults and children who start seeing things differently. The world is moving in a different way, and community organization must constantly evolve in order to keep the land trust in concert with the times.

DAVE SMITH: Do you think it's essential for the community to be the prime mover in creating a community land trust? Or can that come from somewhere else? After you've answered my question, Alejandro, I want to come to Ashley, where a lot of the drive to get the CLT started in Houston came from the city government. First Alejandro, and then over to Ashley. Do you think it's important that the community is there at the very beginning, and are the genesis of the CLT, or can the impetus come from somewhere else, such as a city government?

ALEJANDRO COTTÉ MORALES: A great question. It should be there from the beginning. When we talk about participatory planning, we mean that people should be involved starting from the design phase of their process. Participation makes people feel useful and relevant to the process. Thus, they take responsibility for what happens. If the process is from the top down, if it's implemented incorrectly for lack of active participation, it will not meet the needs of the people; it will not reflect the community's reality.

The community must make the proposals and open up that critical thinking space within the community, so they can design what they need. After that, you need to sit down with the State and the private sector so they can join in the efforts in accordance with the needs of the community. If other people are in charge, the result will not reflect the reality of the community.

DAVE SMITH: Ashley, how do you respond to that? Because no sensible CLT would look a gift horse in the mouth if a city government is looking to help you start.

ASHLEY ALLEN: I would say in our experience, city officials supported the idea of the CLT to get it through city council and to get it funded. They understood, to a certain extent, the community and what they were asking for and what they needed. I will say, however, that there is a challenge when you are funded by city government. Because, one, I don't think any city government has ever been labeled as being efficient, operating efficiently. And, two, city officials aren't on the ground talking to the people.

One of the things that we had to do as an organization was to really get out there and door-knock and have community meetings and have events for people and have meetings with community-based organizations to gather and gain their support. Certain community organizations had already been pushing CLTs. But it had not been widespread. Even though the city was the one to really formulate it, to make it an actual entity, we had to do more work on the back-end to get community support and to get people to understand what a CLT was and why it was beneficial for their community.

It's possible for a CLT to be formulated by, and supported by city government, but I believe the idea and the initial catalyst has to come from the community. If not, then you get the affordable housing programs that we've seen fail over and over and over again. They fail to create a sustainable inventory of affordable housing in cities. So, yes, cities can start it, but the actual organization of the CLT has to come from the wants and the demands of the community. Then you have to follow up and continue to keep the community involved and educated and have their input.

DAVE SMITH: I think that's right. I don't think the organizing work ever really stops.

I want to go to Tony Hernandez on that, because he's got some relevant, first-hand experience here. Tony, we have a phrase in the UK which I think comes from the English Civil War, about the risks of "taking the King's coin." The phrase comes from when people were press-ganged into the King's army. It means that, if you take government money, it comes with a number of strings attached. It strikes me that, in Dudley, you do a lot of good work of balancing the relationship with city government.

TONY HERNANDEZ: I love your quote about "taking the King's coin," but the other quote that you guys have over there is "taking from the rich and giving to the poor." That's the hustle mindset that I work with over here.

The government here in Boston is one that, over 30 years, we've had to build a relationship with. At the beginning, it was all about jumping on them with enough campaigns to get the attention we needed to revitalize our neighborhood. Over time, the City has witnessed the power of the people. They have been more and more willing to come to the table to have discussions with us, versus making decisions for us. The power of the people and raising their voices are things we've continued to elevate. We continue to make sure that's woven into today's organizing.

On occasion, we may have to go old school and do some grassroots organizing. That should never come off the table. But the City understands that we are organized well enough that it'll be rude not to send representatives to have a discussion with us and to figure out how we elevate equity for all. So it's a give and take. You go high, I go low, and let's figure out how to meet in the middle.

DAVE SMITH: We have a question from the audience that I'd like you to address. Do you believe that having eminent domain power in Boston allowed Dudley Neighbors Inc. to develop quicker than other CLTs in the United States?

TONY HERNANDEZ: We used our eminent domain authority as a poking stick. We used it to be able to carve out and get ownership of the land so that we could develop on it. But it was still a grind. Eminent domain allowed us to capture the attention of the owners of parcels of land. You get the attention of the folks that own the land; then you negotiate. We were eventually able to capture the land we have because a foundation granted us about two million dollars. We split that two million into buying these parcels of land. Then we went to developers, engineers, and architects to develop that land.

DAVE SMITH: Geert, I want to come to you, because another thing that community organizers have to do, when negotiating with power, is to make deals, particularly if you're building houses for low-income people. That involves real estate negotiations and transactions. You are an organizer, a brilliant organizer, and someone who's come from a social work background. I wonder, have you or your campaign ever been accused of "selling out," of building homes which are not affordable enough? How do you balance the demands of the communities in which you work with the practical realities of actually trying to get homes built?

GEERT DE PAUW: Well, that's a good question. We had a lot of debates when we started our community land trust. We were in a direct negotiation with the regional government. Something that was crucial for us was to get the support of the government on our issues like who are you building for, who is your target group, how is your board composed? (We really had to struggle not to allow public officials to have a majority on our board.) These issues were very important at the beginning.

Today, the most important objective is to build as many homes as possible and to build them in the best possible way to respond to the needs of the community. What's important there, I think, is that when you start organizing, when you think about the organization, that you do it in a way that you still have this liberty to serve your community.

But I must say, at one point in our history, we were also threatened by the government. Their idea was to incorporate us into an official government program. At that point, really the only moment after the beginning of our community land trust, we really had to restart organizing to show that, for us, it was really important to keep our autonomy.

Do CLT homeowners actually care whether their CLT is community-led?

DAVE SMITH: As we come toward the end of our session, I want to ask you to debate a provocative question. To take the devil's advocate perspective, I want to ask: What difference does it actually make to homeowners who are living in community land trust homes to have a well-organized community around them? It doesn't make their homes warmer. It doesn't make their rent cheaper. Stewardship isn't improved. Why is it essential? Couldn't you just have a decent, benevolent landlord.

So, Tony Hernandez, aren't you spending money on things which aren't improving the lives of the homeowners who are buying your houses?

TONY HERNANDEZ: It's a great question. Now you're giving me a chance to take off my director's cap and to put on my homeowner's cap. As a community land trust homeowner, let me tell you that I've been blessed from day one because of this opportunity for homeownership through a community land trust. It's afforded me the opportunity to grow some equity in my life and for my loved ones to live in a more affordable home. I was able to finish my Master's degree in architecture from Northeastern University. I have a 16-year-old daughter that I've been able to build a 529 college savings account for because of the savings I've been able to realize through homeowner-ship. I'm happy to know that I can pay at least one semester to what-ever college she chooses by the time she's ready to go.

I can't sell my house and make bank because of the limited equity formula, but community land trust homeownership has provided me with so many other open doors and opportunities to build suc-cess for me and my family. And here I am testifying to you folks as a result of that. I'll debate anybody about the blessing that a commu-nity land trust home can bring to their lives.

DAVE SMITH: Ashley, same question to you. I don't know how much money your CLT spends each year on organizing campaigns and the staff responsible for organizing. But if that money was not spent on organizing and built even one extra home, wouldn't that be a greater utility for people in Houston?

ASHLEY ALLEN: What's been mentioned a couple of times is that organizing never stops. Right now, yes, we are in a pretty good space, as we continue to build homes. We are not spending directly on com-munity organizing right now, but we're spending money on com-munity engagement. If we have to come back to the point where we have to organize—and maybe be a little bit more militant in our strategies—we will have an army of people who we've supported and that will now support us.

So we're not spending money on community organizing per se. But community engagement and stewardship? Yes. We're investing heavily in that, because the best organizers, as I mentioned before, are happy homeowners. I want to ensure that our homeowners are in a good space and can talk positively, like Tony just did, about their CLT homeownership experience.

When administrations change, as Alejandro has mentioned, we may not have that support from our city government. We will then have the community fight with us and work with us to gain that sup-port back from our funders, the city government, and foundations and other funding streams, to help the CLT continue to grow. When

you have support of the community, these funders and foundations recognize that, they see that, and they will fund you. So we are
spending right now on stewardship and community engagement for
the purpose of future organizing.

DAVE SMITH: I see. And Alejandro, over to you. You have spent
25 years doing grassroots organizing. Wouldn't it have been better
to have spent that time persuading the government to put a huge
amount of money into your projects? If you had a politician who
could have written a big check, wouldn't that have done so much
more for low-income people than all that community organizing
work in the Caño?

ALEJANDRO COTTÉ MORALES: We have been taught that economic factors move social factors. But when you come from socioeconomic marginalization, you begin realizing that social factors
are what should be moving the economy. In other words, those
rights, the universal right to housing, the right to the land, the right
to health, the right to education, are not negotiable. They can't be
negotiable.

In that sense, everyone has their principles and the things that affected them from a young age. They create the values that guide you
in your community work. When you work with the people, you see
that richness in el barrio, the richness of socially and economically
disadvantaged communities that endure because of their struggle to
survive. The State has never given them anything; all they have, everything that has been accomplished today in our communities, is
the fruit of their efforts and fighting spirit.

So, in that sense, one is not important as a professional. The important thing is for people to bring out their wisdom, that popular
wisdom; to let go of the internalized oppression from all the times
they were told that they are useless. If you're able, you can be a channel, an agitator, an advocate for critical thinking. There is no greater
satisfaction than being part of a collective movement—a movement

that is gaining power and making the State respond as it should, reflecting the reality of the communities and the country as a whole.

Can an organizer also be a developer?

DAVE SMITH: Thank you. And, Geert, my final question to you. What business has a community organizer got going near housing? Developing housing and being a landlord require skilled professionals who know what they're doing, with lawyers and accountants and all those things. How can community organizing be at the heart of a housing offer for people?

GEERT DE PAUW: Well, in our case, we need both. Community organizing was really important at the beginning and today we are we also becoming a housing developer. So we have architects, we have legal people, we have people with financial skills on our team. Without them, nothing would have been built. That's really as crucial as the community organizing.

Community organizing is also very important for us because all of our projects are multi-family homes, with very diverse communities. In order to make them work, it is important to help people get to know each other, to learn how to work together, to learn how to take collective decisions and to do stuff together that has use for the broader community. So, in our case, both are essential to what we do.

DAVE SMITH: That was my final question. Can community organizers also be housing developers? It seems like, for our speakers today, the answer is a resounding yes.

I want to thank everybody on our panel: Ashley Allen of the Houston CLT, Alejandro Cotté Morales of Caño Martín Peña CLT, Geert De Pauw of the Brussels CLT, Tony Hernandez, Dudley Neighbors Inc. And I'm Dave Smith from the London CLT. I'll hand you back to John Davis.

JOHN EMMEUS DAVIS: Thank you Dave, and my thanks to all the

panelists. Practitioner's stories are powerful. They are inspirational. They're informative. We should do more of this sort of thing, telling our stories and sharing our personal experience and organizational experience.

We have just scratched the surface of this important topic. The Center will try to arrange other conversations on this topic in the coming year. We'll find other opportunities for our panelists to delve more deeply into various roles that community organizing can play in "keeping the 'C' in CLT." Good-bye for now.

3.

A Conversation with
Tony Hernandez & Jason Webb,
Dudley Neighbors Inc.

Hosted by María E. Hernández-Torrales
April 4, 2022

MARÍA E. HERNÁNDEZ-TORRALES: Tony and Jason, welcome to this conversation. It is great to have this opportunity to expand on some of the information that you provided last year during the webinars organized by the Center for Community Land Trust Innovation. Tony, you were a panelist in the webinar entitled "CLTs and Community Organizing." And Jason, you were a panelist in the webinar entitled "Building the Beloved Community."

What we want to do, during this dialogue today, is to delve more deeply into the meaning and importance of "community" in the CLT movement. This will be focused on your experience with the Dudley Street Neighborhood Initiative and with Dudley Neighbors Inc. But you may also bring in experiences that you've had in your work with other CLTs.

Let me take a moment to introduce us briefly. Tony Hernandez is a long-time CLT homeowner at Dudley Neighborhoods Inc., the CLT run by DSNI in Boston. He was Executive Director of this CLT until last month. Tony holds a Master's degree in architecture and has long experience in community development and the provision of affordable housing for low-income communities. Jason has served as the Community and Technical Assistance principal at the Grounded Solutions Network. Jason also counts 30 years of experience in community organizing and is a national expert on community land trusts.

As for myself, my name is María E. Hernández-Torrales. I am a lawyer and an adjunct professor at the Community Development Clinic at the University of Puerto Rico School of Law. I've been collaborating for 17 years with the *Fideicomiso de la Tierra del Caño Martín Peña*, also known as the Caño Martín Peña Community Land Trust in San Juan.

Without any further ado, let's get started.

Unpacking the meaning of "community"

MARÍA E. HERNÁNDEZ-TORRALES: A lot of conversations about CLTs assume that everyone who lives in a particular place has the same interests and preferences. Does that reflect the reality of the "community" served by DSNI and DNI?

JASON WEBB: When DSNI was created, it was important that we knew that our community had a lot of different interests at play. We knew there were going to be different sides to how we would deal with the vacant land. But one of the things that the organization's founders quickly realized is, "All right, we need to bring folks together around the commonality that we all share. We all don't like this trash. We all don't like these vacant lots. That's where we need to start building consensus. That's where we need to start building trust, especially across racial groups, especially across different age groups in our community."

The one thing that we all had in common was the fact that a majority of us were poor. This neighborhood here was the only one we could truly afford. But then we also realized through the planning process that there were folks that had wealth in our community, families that passed on their homes, generation after generation. They had generational wealth, because that home was paid off, but that family continued to stay in the community. We had to bring them to the table and say, "Hey, we know that you've been here for a very long time. How can we use the strength of your family's legacy in our community organizing to educate us all to what the community used to be, so we can get a vision for what we want our community to be in the near future?"

That's one of the things that DSNI did extremely well in the 1980s and 1990s when it was preparing its community plan. It would bring in a lot of the seniors to have these talks and say to folks, "I remember when, you know, Dennis Street used to be all sort of triple-deckers and they all had brick façades." Knowing what was here in the past helped newer residents as they were thinking about "Hey, what do we do here? What do we put here?"

I often make the distinction that you have "neighborhoods" and you have "communities." Neighborhoods are those places where people are just living next to each other. Communities are places where you understand that Tony's success is my success; and Tony understands that my failure is part of his failure. We're all interconnected in a certain way. We either all succeed, or we all fail.

Nowadays, I see a lot of people just throwing around "community" and thinking that there's always a community around. I'm of a different mindset, one that says, "No, we have a lot of neighborhoods. But we have very few communities where people actually feel connected to the people living next to them and who actually care about them."

That's something that, you know, this model of a community

land trust needs to elevate. It's not just about homeowners; it's about how those homeowners care about their neighbors, whether or not they're living on a CLT.

TONY HERNANDEZ: I love what Jason says, because I agree with it. Do I want to take care of my family? Absolutely. Do I want to achieve as much success as I can within my lifetime? Absolutely. But, because I live in this neighborhood, I want to think that what I achieve and what I make better in this community has a ripple effect and takes care of my brother, takes care of my sister across the street, a few blocks over. Right? How do I figure out a way to be my brother's keeper and my sister's keeper as a result of whatever personal success I might achieve and whatever involvement I might have in my community?

I think it's a great distinction to make. As Jason said, distinguish between what is a neighborhood and what is a community. A community should have life, should grow, and you should look out for one another. I absolutely agree with that.

But there's a grind to this. In engagements when I'm asked to speak, I like to use the phrase, "If you ain't got love for the game, don't do it." You've got to have love for this game. Right? You've got to have that kind of heart. And if you've got love for the game, then let's work together. Let's make things happen.

MARÍA E. HERNÁNDEZ-TORRALES: You know, there's a saying in the Caño. Before they started this whole project of the community land trust and dredging the channel, people said they were divided by the canal. But now, they say they are united by the canal. They have a vision now, just one vision for the community.

Previously, we used to talk about seven different communities because geographically there are seven neighborhoods, adjacent one to another. But now, we just talk about "the community." This is not to mean they are homogenous. Each has its own, you know, personality. But, still, they are one community because they have one vision for the whole geographic district.

It is very, very important to have this in mind. They are not the same, but they have just one vision for their community. That vision is what keeps them going, as Tony said.

TONY HERNANDEZ: I think that's awesome, María. That's part of what we should strive for in any conversation that touches on this subject. How do you shift mindsets and go from division to unity, creating a common goal? It's okay to agree to disagree. That's perfectly fine. But if you can find commonality, that shifts power. And that's what makes this stuff so exciting to do.

MARÍA E. HERNÁNDEZ-TORRALES: Excellent. Jason, I would like to come back to you in terms of who is served and who is involved in guiding and governing DSNI and DNI. Are there particular income groups or interest groups who are prioritized?

JASON WEBB: The great thing about the Dudley Street story is that, through its design, it is meant to be all-inclusive. We want everybody around the table. We will go the extra mile. We will create the systems and support mechanisms to make sure, for example, that single moms that need childcare can come to a meeting. The organization will make sure to build that into a meeting's design, so that childcare is not a barrier for a community resident to be involved.

We were known, even in the Eighties, as being the most innovative with simultaneous translation. That is now standard in most community meetings throughout the country, but at that time it was groundbreaking that we were doing that.

We were not necessarily thinking about income groups or interest groups. If you are a person who lives in our neighborhood, we want you to be involved. And if you have some wealth, that's great. That means that these meetings are probably going to be easier for you to get to. But if you don't have wealth and you have challenges, come talk to us. We want to take down these barriers, because we want your voice even more.

Then the organization went a step further. We said, "We need the businesses. We need the churches. We need the other nonprofits.

We need all of them around the table." Because from the very beginning, we always looked at Dudley Street as a village. We always hearkened back to that idea that it takes many for a village to thrive.

MARÍA E. HERNÁNDEZ-TORRALES: You say they all have an equal voice?

JASON WEBB: Yes, they definitely have an equal voice. Even in how the Dudley Street Neighborhood Initiative created their board of directors, as groups were starting to wrestle with the racial dynamics in their communities, DSNI very early on was like, "Listen, we're gonna equalize everybody because we want to equalize everybody's voice, bring all of them to the table. We're not gonna do it proportionately to the population, whether there's more African Americans on our board versus white people. We're gonna equalize everybody."

That was a very empowering piece. Residents that came to the table felt like that they were equal with their peers. Yes, maybe 30-40% of the community was African American. But they can still sit at the table with white people, who were only 1% of Dudley's population. You allowed for that equalization, where residents could really focus on, "All right, what's the issue? Well, the issue is that we have too many vacant lots. The issue is that we don't have economic development."

We were not going to allow race and income levels and interest groups to divide us. We knew that we all lived in the same neighborhood. We all suffered the same from these potholes, from these vacant lots. That was the gathering power that sort of created Dudley Street and that, still to this day, propels it.

Cataloguing the benefits of resident engagement

MARÍA E. HERNÁNDEZ-TORRALES: I want to delve more deeply into the rationale for involving residents in the process of planning, guiding, and governing an organization like the CLT in Dudley. Jason, why is community involvement the "right" thing to do?

JASON WEBB: Getting the community involved in any sort of decision-making process of what's going to happen in their own community is definitely the right thing to do, because they're the beneficiaries of it. It affects them every single day of their lives in terms of what's going to happen politically. So, it makes all the sense in the world that you would give power to the people and allow them to make decisions and empower them to go ahead and do that.

For Dudley Street, a lot of the politicians loved the fact that the community was making those decisions, because if anything went wrong the politicians could wipe their hands and say, "Hey, you guys decided that, we didn't."

It was sort of pushing that power to the community and with power comes great responsibility. And practically, it just makes sense. Community involvement needs to be there because they are the ones living there day-to-day.

MARÍA E. HERNÁNDEZ-TORRALES: Thank you. Tony, could you add something to this question too?

TONY HERNANDEZ: This is a conversation that I love having. Unpacking the right ways to move the housing justice needle is always a great conversation to be in.

One of the things that Dudley was able to do was to break the mold on something that had forever had a negative connotation. Prior to DSNI being given the power of eminent domain, there was a negative aura that surrounded that term. But when Dudley got eminent domain, there was the opportunity for many parcels of land to be controlled by the people and not by the government. That was a powerful move, right? That was the true essence of the community, for community, by community.

Piggybacking on what Jason just said, it makes total sense to let the community drive this process. But the opportunity to educate and empower the people on the ground was also a necessity. It didn't happen before, because folks maybe didn't have the education or didn't feel empowered enough to really want to take over a process like this. For a regular guy, it could be a scary thing.

María E. Hernández-Torrales: Tony, I want to continue with you. What are the benefits for the organization when involving residents?

Tony Hernandez: Well, the organization has the opportunity to gain trust and to build a relationship with people who are part of that community. I mentioned that you want to educate folks, but you also want to empower them. One of the things that has gotten lost in our world historically, when it comes to how we live in our neighborhoods, is the opportunity of control: having a seat at the table, having a community that feels empowered and educated to a degree that they can come to a space and offer their voices and opinions.

In the past, it's always been a top-down process, while the community was fighting for a bottom-up process. At Dudley, we're finding a way to meet in the middle. Don't exclude the community. Find a way to work from the bottom-up and let the top-down work its process, so that everyone has a seat at the table.

An organization like DSNI acts, kind of symbolically, as a doctor whose responsibility is to capture the vitals of the community: taking the pulse of the community; having a diagnostic of what's really going on, versus someone else coming in and thinking, "Oh, you're this sick, so let's give you this kind of medicine."

María E. Hernández-Torrales: Jason, do you have any thoughts about the benefits of community involvement for the organization?

Jason Webb: I would say that an organization like a CLT continues to be grounded when you have resident participation. For Dudley Street, the organization was initially created by folks that did not live in that community. The organization then took a very different turn when power was given to people who actually lived there. The organization started to get more buy-in from other residents because they saw their neighbors being empowered, their neighbors being in leadership, their neighbors actually doing some of the work that propelled the organization.

MARÍA E. HERNÁNDEZ-TORRALES: This is very important. I can recall when the Caño communities started organizing in San Juan, there were like 12 community leaders involved. By the present time, we have 120 leaders, not to mention many other people who get involved. We are very convinced that the organization benefits a lot from community participation.

I would like to continue with Jason. For people who live in the Dudley neighborhood who do not live on the CLT's land, what are the benefits for them?

JASON WEBB: I've always felt like, with a community land trust, you cannot provide benefits just for your homeowners. As a CLT, you really have to take community as far and wide as possible and be inclusive of everybody. Whether they're homeowners who are on your land, or whether they're private individuals living next to it, everyone gains. Everyone gains from the efforts of the CLT.

For Dudley Street, it was transformative taking blocks of our neighborhood that may have only had one home on them and literally building around those remaining houses. Also, at the same time, we were engaging those homeowners to make sure they had enough yard space, that they had enough space around their homes, as we were building, to make sure they had a comfort level with development.

When it comes to economics, homeowners in the neighborhood who are not on the CLT's land but who see improvements from new CLT homes being built, probably see their property values increase. Instead of having vacant lots or burned-out shells of houses, there is actually something in the neighborhood that has value. Plus, you have additional neighbors and more eyes on the street to help deal with any public nuisance issues that may come up. You also have an organization that is built around the premise that the entire community needs to advance, needs to prosper. The organization is not there just for the residents living on the CLT's land, but for all the residents around the CLT's land.

That's why, at least for Dudley, we did a lot of work in making sure that, as we did a lot of stewardship for our homeowners, at specific times we also allowed for that stewardship to flow to their neighbors. If we were bringing in a contractor, let's say a fencing contractor, and some of the neighbors also wanted their fencing done, we didn't say, "Oh no, these fencing contractors can only work for our homeowners." We would share that information and allow for those other homeowners to share in some of benefits we were bringing in.

TONY HERNANDEZ: I want to piggyback on what Jason just pointed out about non-CLT homeowners benefitting from all the resources that we try to bring to our homeowners living on the land trust. We bring in quality contractors. We bring in quality plumbers and electricians. We want to ensure that folks aren't getting hustled in terms of the pricing they're paying for home improvements. We fight for them, right? The nature of the CLT model is to fight against speculation and gentrification in an entire neighborhood. It isn't just for the benefit of those that are on the land trust's lands, but also for those that are living in the neighborhood in market-rate homes.

This is the equation that the model looks to balance out, right? On a day-to-day basis, how do we allow a neighborhood to grow in a fair manner: not to have people get bought out by speculators; not to have people get pushed out because of the lack of affordability in the neighborhood.

The model looks to preserve this old-school feel of a village, a place where your children can play outside and your neighbors are watching over them when you cannot. The essence of that lies in weaving all of these pieces together. Whether you have a market-rate home or a community land trust home, the goal is that we ultimately share those resources and those benefits, so at the end of the day we can live successful lives with our families. I would like to think that's the main goal of a CLT.

Of course, everyone wants to get ahead as individuals, everyone wants to gain more riches. But, at the end of the day, you want to live a life. You want to raise your children. You want to be happy, right? And this model, I think, has benefits not only for community land trust homeowners, but also for those who have nothing to do with the CLT. They are welcome to share in the riches that come from community.

María E. Hernández-Torrales: At the Caño, it's a little bit different. In our informal settlement we have like 50% who are private homeowners and 50% who are people who live within the community land trust. So maybe I am a private homeowner, but my neighbor lives on community land trust land. So, 50% have title to the land. The other 50% don't, who we call "persons of interest." And these people are invited to our general meetings for the community land trust. They receive the same information, as Jason was saying. They know about everything because they were also in danger of being displaced because of the dredging of the channel. They will also be affected by the infrastructure programs and everything that is happening in the Caño, which is happening for the benefit of the whole community.

Tony, I would like to ask you, as a homeowner within the community land trust in Dudley, could you tell us what difference, if any, does it make to have a well-organized community around you?

Tony Hernandez: Well, it's the difference between receiving certain benefits when city or state funding is being allocated, whether for development, or for education, or for street sweeping in the neighborhood. The benefit of being organized is that of being paid attention to by government.

I grew up in low-income neighborhoods in Boston. So I know what it's like to live in neighborhoods that get ignored. And now, in my experience, I can see what an organization like the Dudley Street Neighborhood Initiative can do as a facilitator, as an advocate for justice towards housing, for justice towards workforce development, for justice towards healthy eating initiatives. It makes a difference having a voice and an advocate that can elevate our neighborhood in the eyes of government to assure we're being served.

MARÍA E. HERNÁNDEZ-TORRALES: Excellent. Jason, would you like to add something? You started in this movement very early in your life. You now have 30 years of experience with CLTs.

JASON WEBB: Being part of an organized community is understanding the power dynamics, as Tony said, making sure that you get the same services as other communities. Those other communities, unfortunately, sometimes wield power with the checkbook. They are able to make large donations to political campaigns, so their needs get met by those politicians. But in low-income communities, the biggest tools they have are collaboration and invoking their power through the ballot box. Certain politicians know that when you go into a well-organized community, they need to mind their Ps and Qs because they understand that, "Hey, I work for these people."

When they're well-organized, residents can go to the organization in their community and get the organization to stick its head out there and to wield its weight. It's not up to any individual to do it.

That's very important, because we have seen how governments can clap back on lower-income communities and individuals and give them a penalty for speaking out. But when you're in a well-organized community that has a vehicle of an organization like DSNI to do that advocacy, it's very hard for a government to do that.

Dealing with divisions within Dudley

MARÍA E. HERNÁNDEZ-TORRALES: My next question is about dealing with divisions within your "well-organized community." What if some residents want the CLT to do one thing and other residents want you to do something else?

TONY HERNANDEZ: Well, we go through what I think is a fair, democratic process. We have community meetings. We have a committee called the Sustainable Development Committee within the Dudley Street Neighborhood Initiative. It's a committee designed to bring the community together, to talk about development in the neighborhood. At those meetings we bring developers and we bring architects, engineers. And they do presentations.

We've had many presentations where a developer shows up and says that they're bringing million-dollar condominiums into the neighborhood. And everybody in the room's kind of like, "I can't afford a million-dollar condominium. That's ultimately going to cause a rise in my rent or prices are going to go up in the neighborhood and I won't be able to live here anymore."

I've been in plenty of meetings where there are disagreements between what folks think should be affordable and what isn't affordable; how much parking there is and how much parking there isn't going to be; who gets to live there; who gets priority in buying those units.

So, you do find moments where there are disagreements between community members. I know a lot of folks shy away from what sometimes feels contentious. Right? But for me, it feels fine. It's okay to have contention in a room, so long as you're navigating through that dynamic in a manner that isn't harmful to anyone.

There's a level of respect that you have to maintain. We go through a democratic process of voting, where majority votes are what ends up being where you choose which way you want to go. But you lay ground rules prior to that democratic process to establish an understanding of how you will move in a meeting space.

For our Sustainable Development Committee meetings, we establish simple rules like there's one mic. You don't want two, three, ten people talking at the same time. Let's respect one another and have one mic at a time. And learn to step up and step back. There are folks that are more vocal than others, and they tend to speak up more. If you've spoken too much, learn to step up and take a step back so that others can have an opportunity to get their voice on the table. And we will agree to disagree. Everybody in this space is not going to agree to the same thing. Let's agree to disagree and be adults about it. Right?

On occasion, you're going to have folks that won't follow the rules, so you learn to work through that dynamic and still push through a democratic process that achieves a majority vote and establishes where the majority of the community wants to move. You learn to respect that opinion of the community.

MARÍA E. HERNÁNDEZ-TORRALES: Jason, could you tell us about your experience with division?

JASON WEBB: I'll hearken back to a situation we had with a bodega's storeowners, who wanted to bring in beer and wine. They were going in front of the City of Boston's Licensing Committee and that Committee wanted to hear from us at the Dudley Street Neighborhood Initiative. What did we feel about it? Were we going to support it or decline it?

The storeowners came in to DSNI and walked through their idea, "Hey, financially, what's going to keep us open is the ability for us to bring in beer and wine to help supplement everything else that we're selling."

The Sustainable Development Committee was completely split. We had invited residents from the area around the store to come to say their piece and they were also completely split. That's because alcohol consumption was a real concern. In our community, it felt like you had a liquor store on every block. That's something that the residents there and the Committee were really grappling with. They understood that this store owner might not be able to keep their doors open without this. But, at the same time, they didn't want to continue to allow this to happen in our community. What's the right decision?

It literally took a six-month process of this storeowner coming back, and the Committee saying, "You know what? We will let you to do beer and wine, but we don't want any nips, any small containers. We want you to promise that you're going to keep your store completely clean. And we want you to go to this park down the street and commit to cleaning up that park every week, because our fear is that people are going to buy stuff from your store, go down to the park, consume it, and just leave the cans there."

The storeowner agreed to everything. Then a nearby neighborhood association said, "No, zero tolerance, no more alcohol in our community." And the Sustainable Development Committee deferred to this neighborhood association because they were closer. And the storeowner understood. "All right. You guys ran us through the process. We agreed to all these things. But we understand that you're going to defer to this other group."

Unfortunately, they had to close their store after a year, because they just couldn't keep up with the smaller revenue coming in. And then, a few years later, the chair of that neighborhood association was complaining that she didn't have access to food and that DSNI needed to advocate for a store. I sat down with her and said, "You know, we had an opportunity to keep a relatively community-minded storeowner here, if we were just willing to concede a little bit. That storeowner was willing to do other things that you guys wanted, but you guys had the zero tolerance for alcohol."

That store has now gone through different hands, and the current owners are not community-minded. They're like, "Hey, we just want to take our money, lock up, and that's it. No, we're not going to donate to your cleanup. No, we're not going to try to run for your board. We don't even live here. We don't care."

That, to me, was a really good lesson. You can run the greatest process ever, but sometimes a decision still needs to be unpacked a little bit more. If we had given it a little bit more time, we would've realized that it wasn't a whole community association decision that was being made. It was one individual in the association who had a personal bias against alcohol and who was willing to wield her power to basically stop a community storeowner from succeeding.

This idea of community is not always a bunch of roses. Some of this stuff is really, really messy.

María E. Hernández-Torrales: Yes. It is.

Tony Hernandez: Jason makes a great point. It's important to identify, right off the cuff, those who are willing to work with the community and those who are not. Right? There are those who have an obvious agenda of making as much money as they can. That is not to say there can't be a transformative moment that turns a business that was all about the money into one that is now also benefitting those less fortunate in the neighborhood they're running a business in. In the midst of this dynamic that Jason speaks of, we don't want to forget the opportunities for transformative moments.

Then again, there are those who refuse to budge on helping the community. And that's when you go old school. When someone has made it clear that they intend to bring no benefit to a community that is underserved, you go to the grassroots level, you show up at the zoning hearings, you show up at the city council meetings with a crowd of people and you protest against whatever development is happening in your neighborhood. Weaving through that dynamic is incredibly important.

Partnering with "outsiders"

María E. Hernández-Torrales: Jason, my next question is for you. Have any people who live outside of your CLT's service area played essential roles in establishing and expanding the CLT?

Jason Webb: When folks ask, "How have you been so successful?" I've always said, "One, community—a community staying strong and staying together—and, two, the City."

Our biggest partner was city government. I used to call them the "lovely bureaucrats." They didn't live in our community, but they felt a very special connection to our community. I remember one of our senior program officers, Christine O' Keith. Christine and I did about five different housing developments together. (When I initially came into Dudley Street, we were working on Tony's home.) Just the love and passion that she would put into these projects. For her, it wasn't like, "Oh yeah, this is just another development that I'm pushing paper for." She would be like, "Hey, how can we do this better? How can we improve?" So, definitely, outside folks were needed.

The other large contributor to our success was our legal firm, Goulston-Storrs, in Boston, Massachusetts. Over the years, I would say they have probably contributed at least a million dollars' worth of services to our community, through their expertise of knowing the law and representing our CLT.

I say to a lot of start-up CLTs, never take for granted a great law firm that is comfortable walking into City meetings and having relationships with City Attorneys. Those City Attorneys knew, "All right, we're trusting in this group because they've got a really good counsel." And, you know, some of those agreements would have been deal-breakers. But the lawyers were able to hash it out and basically make it so that it was a win-win.

The other outsider, who built most of the homeownership units on our CLT, was a private developer. He was part of a very small development team that came into our community and basically said, "We don't live here, but we really like your community. We like your community because we know that we're gonna get political kudos for working with you guys." But the second thing they said is that they would not put any type of building material into our homes that they wouldn't put into the million-dollar condos that they were building in the South End.

I know a number of communities think, "We don't want anybody or any help from the outside." For me, that's the wrong perspective.

If you get people who believe in the mission, who believe in the vision and come with an open heart, the community should consider working with them.

MARÍA E. HERNÁNDEZ-TORRALES: Tony, what are your thoughts about this?

TONY HERNANDEZ: I like to think that, in the years that I've practiced, now well over two decades, I've not excluded anyone who had an interest in helping to move this agenda forward. Obviously we want the locals; and the governing structure that we have set up here in Dudley has a particular catchment area and only people who live in that catchment area are allowed to run for the board that makes up the governing structure of the organization.

Nonetheless, with open arms I welcome anyone who has love for the game, whether that's a financial institution, a foundation, attorneys, or colleges and universities. That also includes other nonprofit organizations that are looking to understand how this process works. We've been accepting of all of that—and their help is crucial. There's power in numbers, so I don't think we've ever turned away any such help.

I'm of the mindset that we accept everyone and anything that comes our way. Part of my job as the director of DNI was always to analyze whether there was good or bad behind whoever was coming our way. Was this going to benefit our people? Was it going to benefit our program? Did it align with our mission and values? If so, we were in the same boat as far as I was concerned.

But if it would take away from the mission and the values and the directive that I'd been given to run this organization and to grow it and to steward it in a positive way, then my job was to say, "No, that's as far as you go."

You know, there are people that have participated in the work that we've done over the years who have a love for the game. And thank goodness for those folks. However, let's not pay attention just to all the shine of the story. There are also folks that still don't care much for the community benefit, don't care much for the fact that they're serving underserved people. Right? Their focus is still about making money and walking away with fat pockets.

This ain't checkers, let's play chess. Sometimes making strategic moves in the midst of this work are things that I've practiced. I've worked with folks that I can tell don't give a damn about what the community's going to benefit from. That's okay, if what you're contributing to the community is going to help the less fortunate. If you think you're walking away with some kudos at a city level, okay that's cool, but we're gonna hold your feet to the fire if you come back to Dudley. You're gonna bring something to the community that's going to be a benefit.

JASON WEBB: That's right.

TONY HERNANDEZ: You have to understand how to play the game of chess with these folks and leverage whatever it is that they can bring. They might not have love for the game, I dare say, but that's all right if, at the end of the day, they're helping the less fortunate and pushing our mission and values forward. I've spoken with communities in other cities that said, "But we can't work with our elected officials. We can't work with the City." I say, "Well, you gotta find a way to build a strategy into that conversation." Work out a strategy, right? That's just a part of this game, unfortunately, whenever we try to bring justice to the less fortunate. That's a part of this grind, a part of this hustle.

MARÍA E. HERNÁNDEZ-TORRALES: That's good.

JASON WEBB: It truly is, Tony. And I think even the grittier piece of all this is how do you also work with other nonprofits that are based in your neighborhood? What if they just want to make money to keep their doors open, but they don't necessarily care about the community? They just need that development so they can get their fee, so that they can keep their staff going. But do they care about quality? No. Do they care if the project's actually gonna get done in a timely way? No. Do they care about hiring people in the community? No. These are all things that we have come across.

When DSNI was started, we were created by a bunch of community development corporations that saw a large funder that wanted to fund a new initiative. And these same developers, these same community development corporations, none of their executive directors lived in the community. And our founding residents questioned them and said, "Why haven't you helped our community before? Why are you just coming to the table now—because there's money?"

Those things are real in a lot of communities, where you have a community development corporation and they're the only game in town. How do you play that chess game with them?

One of the sad parts of our organization's story, from my perspective, is that we got sold a bill of goods in the development of the Kroc Center. We, as a community, let our guard down and allowed a very large nonprofit, the Salvation Army, to come in and use us. We didn't think that a religious nonprofit organization would ever do that and, boy, were we wrong. There were battles which ensued during construction and after construction over promises that were made by the Salvation Army prior to construction even happening. We didn't put anything in writing; we just took their word for it. We wouldn't have done that for any other developer that would have come to us. But for some reason, we let that developer take us all by surprise and they didn't live up to most of their promises.

Overcoming barriers to participation

MARÍA E. HERNÁNDEZ-TORRALES: Wow, excellent example. Let's move to the last part of our conversation. I want to ask about the obstacles to getting residents involved in planning, guiding, and governing the organization in Dudley. And what strategies have proven to be the most effective in overcoming those obstacles to keep the flame of participation alive?

JASON WEBB: It's a challenge getting residents to come out and actually participate. You know, we never did the sort of classic Saul Alinsky organizing, where there always needed to be a boogeyman; there always needed to be a target. Our organizing principle came from a more participatory and common-vision standpoint. We looked at it like, "Hey, everybody in this community matters; we have a vision; and the residents here should be the primary decision makers." The big thing that our organization really wanted to do was to give folks the vocabulary, the skills, and the confidence to be able to walk into any sort of planning meeting and feel like they were equal to any professional in the room. The goal was to build leaders, and then for those leaders to cultivate the new leaders.

I started doing this work at seven years old, volunteering at the organization. Our first big thing was neighborhood cleanups, which a lot of the youth loved to do. That gave us an opportunity to clean a piece of vacant land in our community and then to say, "What should go there?" And DSNI would say, "If you want to have that discussion, you should come to our meetings." We would walk into these meetings, but it was just an adult conversation. So a lot of youth would go in the room and just be silent and just absorb.

You know, it's one hurdle to get residents that may not understand a financial statement to learn how to actually learn that skill. But it's a totally different thing when you've got a 14-year-old or a 16-year-old sitting in the board meeting. And you've got adults talking and throwing out acronyms all over the place. And that youth member is like, "What the heck did I get myself into?!?"

Some youth would easily be deterred by that, but there were adults in the room who recognized that and said, "Hey, I'm gonna take you under my wing. And any questions you have, I'm gonna sit next to you and we'll sort of go back and forth. Or I can break things down for you in real time. If you do have a question, you can feel confident in going ahead and asking it."

It's those things, making sure that you actually have a very deliberate way of saying that every resident should have a seat at the table, and it's our job to make sure that there are no barriers to them getting to that seat.

That was a lot, in the early beginnings of the Dudley Street Neighborhood Initiative, that was really looked at, "How do we remove some of these barriers?" I'm assuming that Tony can talk a lot more about the current day of what those barriers are, and how he and his team have been able to overcome them.

MARÍA E. HERNÁNDEZ-TORRALES: Tony, please.

TONY HERNANDEZ: How do we do this today versus ten or thirty years ago? I think that the internal structure isn't too different. The constant variables are what I call it the Triple E's: Engagement, Education, and Empowerment. So long as you're engaging with the community, then you're finding a way to bring them to the table; and you're finding a way to educate them; and you're finding a way to empower them. If you're continuing that level of communication and conversation, the rest should fall in place.

We inherited a world where there had been a lot of grassroots organizing. You had pioneers like Jason literally picking up a rake, picking up a broom, and physically cleaning up a dirty lot because our neighborhood physically needed that level of improvement. Right?

We evolved to a place where technology began to take off, and we're able now to create fliers and post fliers and make phone calls and let folks know that, you know, the monthly Sustainability Committee meeting is happening on the fourth Thursday of every month.

And then COVID happens and it pretty much threw a curve ball to the planet, where folks had to remain in place. We had to reinvent ourselves when it came to community organizing. We took a pause at Dudley when COVID hit. I could see it in the staff's faces of like, "Wait a minute. We're so used to engaging physically with the community and having gatherings with people. What happens when you remove that rug from underneath us?" Everything suddenly relied on learning how to master zoom. And the world of video conferencing took off because of COVID.

We found ways to reinvent ourselves. Again, engage, educate, and empower the community, right? Like, I'm looking at you through a screen, nice folks. But the ability to make that connection is still the key. It doesn't matter what the structure or technology might be, so long as you're able to do that engagement, that education, that empowerment of the people.

Keeping the flame of participation alive

MARÍA E. HERNÁNDEZ-TORRALES: How do you keep the flame of participation alive?

TONY HERNANDEZ: It's about relationships, María. I don't want to run into Jason once a month for a check-in, but I do want to wish him a Merry Christmas. On Thanksgiving I want to send him a nice note. On Halloween maybe his kids will see my kids, trick-or-treating down the street. You want to build relationships with people.

I love the way Jason phrased it earlier. If you can find a way to live in a community instead of in a neighborhood, that part takes care of itself. You build relationships. It isn't always going to be about, "Are you going to the meeting?" It may be about, "Okay María, I'm sorry, you ran out of rice? I've got an abundance of rice at the house, so I'll bring some over to you." I'm building a relationship with you, letting you know that I want to take care of you.

It isn't purely about the work. It's about building those relationships. There are times when I purposely do not talk about the work. Right? I ask them, "How are you? How's your family? What's going on in your life? What's new and exciting?" Let's build the relationship so that it doesn't feel like business every time we have an encounter. It feels like we're one big family. On occasion, yes, family business has to be handled. But on other occasions? Let's just be family. Let's have a cookout. You swing by and I happen to be cooking in the back yard, stop by for a burger. Right? Have a beer, have a soda. That sort of relationship building is important in the midst of this work.

JASON WEBB: To piggyback on what Tony just said, there was the fact that our organization did not just look at Dudley and say, "Oh, we just want to build housing." We also wanted to involve people in designing and building outside spaces that can be in complement to the housing. For Dudley Street, we have several town commons. The design of those spaces was for residents to come together, to enjoy music. One of our nonprofit partners, The Food Project, uses a lot for their farmers market, which brings an additional sort of service to our community. We have developed, you know, playgrounds. We've developed orchards. We've developed community gardens. We've developed a 10,000-square-foot community greenhouse. These are additional facilities and assets of the community, where residents can gather.

One of the things that is absolutely true is what Tony said about relationship building. That's why, after they move into the CLT, sometimes even before all the homeowners get into their homes, you bring them together so they know their new neighbors. You also make sure that new residents understand that they're walking into a community. So your participation is going to be a little bit different than if you were just moving into a neighborhood.

I always used to say to folks that used to compliment us and say, "Wow, you guys have done amazing stuff. How are you able to sell these homes so quickly?" And I'd tell them, "I don't just sell homes, I sell a home within a community."

Every year, DSNI puts together a multicultural festival to really help residents to come out and celebrate the diversity of the community. It is a celebration. It is one of those things where, again, we're able to create spaces that allow for these festivals to happen. We also bring folks together throughout the year so there's a constant communication, constant relationship building. Because that's what's going to build trust, and that's what's ultimately going to build power.

TONY HERNANDEZ: On the topic of relationship building, you know that during the pandemic everything got shut down. Everyone was told to pretty much stay home. I met up with my staff. One of the things that I instructed my staff to do, including myself, was that we were going to divide up the names of every homeowner on the land trust and we were going to give each of them a phone call. I said, "We're going to give them a phone call, and we're going to conduct an extremely simple, two-question survey. "How are you? What do you need?" Very simple, right?

We got donations of money that we turned into gift cards and gave to our homeowners, whenever we got those allotments of money. The Food Project teamed up with us and we built bags of produce. We got boxes of canned, non-perishable food from the City of Boston and the Food Pantry here in Boston.

And, you know, my staff put me to work as well. During Thanksgiving, I think I stopped at close to 20 front porches of community land trust homeowners to drop off boxes of food and produce, because we had folks that either couldn't come out or had a fear of coming out.

And let me tell you, I enjoyed every single visit, the feeling of dropping off a box of food and a bag of produce on someone's front porch. Ringing their doorbell, running back down the steps, and from the sidewalk seeing them open the door. They'd recognize me and knew that I was from the land trust. Then I'd say, "There you go, and I hope you enjoy it." And the smile on their faces made all the difference for me. It was worth the trip. It was worth driving around the neighborhood, dropping off food for folks that were in need.

So we found ways to build those relationships and to keep in contact with folks, even in the midst of COVID.

Balancing the roles of organizer and developer

María E. Hernández-Torrales: I have one last question for you both. Is there a tension between keeping up with the organizing work and fulfilling your responsibilities as a developer? Do you feel any tension playing both of those roles?

Tony Hernandez: Yeah. I'd be lying if I said there wasn't any tension in trying to carry out the responsibilities of being a developer, while making sure there's a seat at the table for everyone. In my experience, having been involved with this community in Dudley for over 20 years, having previously managed multi-million-dollar projects for an architectural firm for 13 years, and having worked in multiple communities throughout the United States, I can say there's a role for everyone to play.

But juggling multiple roles can get really thin at times; things can fall through the cracks. In my line of work, supervising Dudley Neighbors, there have been times when I could have just put on my project manager's cap, but we also needed to organize. We also needed to bring the people together. We needed to have conversations with the City. We needed to work with the banks and the attorneys. There are multiple things to juggle. You have to learn to let others lead in the skill sets that they're good at, and contribute to the greater good.

MARÍA E. HERNÁNDEZ-TORRALES: Excellent. Jason.

JASON WEBB: So the Dudley Street Neighborhood Initiative was set up with this question in mind. It's no accident that the land trust is a separate organization from the organizing and planning agency. Remember, at Dudley Street, you have two 501(c)(3) nonprofits: one's a land trust; and the other's about organizing and planning. That was by design. We wanted to allow for organizers and planners to do their thing. Don't worry about development; our development arm will implement what you guys come up with.

The other great thing about Dudley Street is that the land trust had to get into being the developer on only a few occasions. We usually partnered with developers. And that team would put the land trust in a more powerful position because we were owning land that they developing on.

There were tensions in a lot of our developments, but the tension was more because a developer had to understand a new way of doing development where they didn't hold all the power. They had to work with the land trust and, because it's our land, you're going to do exactly what we tell you to do. If there's a problem, you're not just going to come up with a solution by yourself. You're going to bring the CLT in and get our opinion on how to resolve this issue. The developer and their architects just couldn't be making decisions without us at the table, because that was our land.

That was one of the big reasons why, for the CLT, we would ground lease our land to the developer. We wanted to put the developer on a certain playing field where we get to sign off on their product. We're not just going to accept anything they build.

TONY HERNANDEZ: I love that my predecessors at Dudley made the decision to create two different nonprofits. That was a great move in avoiding certain tensions. I've used it to my benefit in playing good-cop/bad-cop. There were moments when I could purely wear that bad-cop hat and say, "This is how it's going to go, because these are the instructions that the community has provided; this is what they want to see as an outcome; this is my charge."

The organizing arm of the organization can build the relationships and leverage power and protest, while the land trust, as owner of the land, can work with the developer and say, "Well, you know, the community wants to see x, y, and z."

The tensions will be inevitable, but how do you address them? Right? We're going to move through this strategically, we're going to move through this democratically. What we want to do is sit at the table together and have a conversation about this. But also understand that, if you refuse to work with us, the people will find a way to make you do whatever it is you need to do for our neighborhood. We use it as a poking stick.

MARÍA E. HERNÁNDEZ-TORRALES: Jason, you were going to add something.

JASON WEBB: Yeah, I was just going to elevate what Tony was saying. A number of other communities in Boston used to get upset that Dudley Street always got pretty much everything that we wanted from the City. One of the things that we would say to these other communities is, "We don't rush to protest. We rush to find commonality with City folks. We don't walk into the room and feel like, 'Oh, you guys have wronged us.'" We would walk into the room being partnership-ready. That's the reason that you get what you want without needing to protest.

That's something that a number of communities still have a long way to learn. Yes, cities across this country have always shafted lower-income communities and neighborhoods. That's a fact. But that sort of history should not drive your tactics when City officials want to come back around to work with you.

One of the biggest barriers that I've seen with a number of communities is that they are too scarred by the past to be open to what a different future could be. You know, in Dudley, half of our land was vacant. The City allowed for dumping to happen widely. And our residents were like, "You know what? This sucks, but we're not going to keep this chip on our shoulder. There are too many things to do. The City? How can we get a place at the table and how can we work as partners, not as adversaries?" We're not going to run in there and start screaming and yelling and saying that these people have wronged us. We're going to walk in and say, "Hey, this is the problem. How can we all solve it?"

You know, there's still a lot of things that Dudley Street can go ahead and protest about to this day. But they're wise enough to say, "You know what? That's not a winning strategy. A better strategy is for us to get the right partners at the table and to figure out a solutions-based way of correcting this, not a we-need-somebody-to-blame type of strategy."

María E. Hernández-Torrales: Thank you so much, Jason. Thank you so much, Tony. We should probably stop here. I am appreciating very much your time, and I appreciate all your knowledge. It's been such a good conversation. Thank you so much.

TONY HERNANDEZ: I appreciate you having me, María, and, I think the conversation about the place of community in our work must continue to be unpacked. And we need to continue to unpack our conversation today and find ways to substantiate some of these things and make them real, so that others can carry this baton forward, whenever we are ready to put that baton down. I know I'm not ready to put mine down as yet. Jason, I'm sure you're not, either. Neither are you, María!

JASON WEBB: That's true! Thank you, María, for your time.

4.

A Conversation with
Razia Khanom & Dave Smith,
London Community Land Trust

Hosted by Greg Rosenberg
March 30, 2022

GREG ROSENBERG: Razia and Dave, thank you for participating in this conversation. I've been a huge fan from afar of the London CLT—and of your predecessor organization, the East London CLT. This is a big treat for me.

I want to start with the rationale for involving residents in the first place. So my first question for you is why is community involvement the "right" thing to do, morally, politically, or practically? Who wants to take a shot at that?

DAVE SMITH: I'm going to let Razia answer this question first. (That's what we call in rugby a "hospital pass.") Also, I got paid to work on the London CLT, in the first instance. Razia came to it, presumably, because she believed it was the right thing to do. So it seems only right that I let her start.

RAZIA KHANOM: Thank you Dave. You're very lucky you got paid to do it. It means that you had the freedom to actually spend all your daytime doing that. But I genuinely think that your passion mirrors my own.

Why is it the right thing to do? Our survival as human beings has been built on community, from way back when we were cavemen and women. Bringing it up to modern times, we see the effects when we don't work as communities and what happens to communities and how they begin to disintegrate.

We are very lucky that there are some people like Dave who are paid to do it, and others who give up their free time to do it. Because if we had not been around, we would all feel the effects of not taking part in community work. We all benefit from taking part in such work—socially, economically, mentally. To feel safe, to feel secure, underpins the healthy existence of everybody around us. Why is it the right thing to do? It would be foolish for us not to do it.

Like Dave said, it's a passion of mine. Because I see what inadequate housing and inadequate social and community work does to a community. It's heartbreaking.

Sometimes people can be scared off into not taking part, because we're all expected to do the same thing. But it's when all those individual pieces and different levels of community work come together to create a package that we thrive. We all thrive off the back of that.

DAVE SMITH: I should qualify my answer by saying that, whilst I was paid to lead the London CLT, I wasn't paid very much to do it!

GREG ROSENBERG: [laughs]. That's good. That's good.

DAVE SMITH: Without getting too deep into the etymology of "morally," I think it's important to hold democratic participation as a moral virtue, as a moral value. In the context of the UK at least, we have market provision of housing and we have state provision of housing. Both of them have fallen short, morally—albeit in different ways.

The case for market housing falling short is just unarguable, as far as I'm concerned. The case for the state provision of housing falling short morally is a more difficult one, but I think it is the case. Over time, the structures that arose—bureaucratic and unrepresentative—caused a form of moral deficit in the way in which we manage our affordable housing stock.

I think there is a need for greater participation in the way in which we deliver affordable housing. The CLT brings the best of those two worlds, as well as bringing with it a more participatory form, which I personally think is a moral virtue.

Politically, participation was essential for us. The London CLT would not have happened otherwise; this kind of housing doesn't happen otherwise. The market and the state leave this hole, which London CLT steps forward to fill.

The old organizing slogan is that, "If one person has got a problem, it's their problem; but if 100 people have got a problem, it's our problem." Or at least it's the politician's problem. That's why community involvement is important politically. Certainly in the case of St. Clements, it wouldn't have happened without our politics forcing the political will. It was only because we were knocking on the door of city hall that it eventually happened.

And practically, community involvement is important because it just builds better places for people to live. I really do believe that. We need planning experts and we need architects. They're brilliant, important people. But they can benefit hugely, like any profession does, from the lived experience of the users.

Nowhere is this lived experience more important than in housing. Yet the housing industry, by and large, doesn't put much time and effort into understanding their consumer base. It's purely there just to provide a product which is fairly standard, driven by averages in terms of what people want and monetized in terms of minimum floor space and the most the industry can charge.

Razia can actually speak to this far better than me in practical terms of building communities that represent ways of living that are different than traditional, white, working-class ways of living in the East End. This can have a huge influence on the houses that we build and on the communities that are built on the back of them.

RAZIA KHANOM: Absolutely, absolutely. Going back a little further in history, I think it's interesting that we saw one of the biggest, most ambitious housing drives, post-Second World War. We also saw the introduction of the NHS. We invested in our communities. It was not just market housing. Social housing and housing associations were created to serve the needs of individual communities.

When we stopped doing that, we saw things diluted. It took away from understanding those individual communities, because when those communities thrive in their identities and in their safe space you get that burst of diversity and appreciation for all walks of life.

It was in the 1980s, I think, when the housing policy changed. Since then, we haven't seen adequate housing. Locally there are 36,000 people in my borough that are on housing waiting lists; 36,000 people! For far too long, we haven't had enough politicians on the same page. It's that disconnect which London CLT does an amazing job of addressing, actually finding solutions which take into account not just housing needs, but all the other elements that tie in with that.

Organizing continues after a CLT is established

GREG ROSENBERG: So, let me ask you this. At this point, London CLT has a pretty good idea of what the needs of its community are, right? Why does it benefit the organization to continue your community organizing activities?

RAZIA KHANOM: I'm going to step in here and say that, technically, we're not the organization as such. We are representatives who have been elected by our membership. We're extensions of that community. Why does it benefit us? Because we are part of that membership, we are part of those communities. When we're presenting ourselves to key partners, we're an organization. But we are actually, in essence, still in that community, all those communities combined. So why? In benefiting the organization, it is directly benefiting us and our communities. We're one and the same.

DAVE SMITH: Yeah, I'd go along with that. There are some really practical examples of why community involvement is immediately worthwhile to us, as London CLT. One, this work gets easier when you make your peace with the fact that it never stops. You never reach a stage where you're like, "Oh, we're done." If we're building new sites to fund the organization and to further our mission, we can't start every time from nowhere and say, "Oh, we need to do some community organizing work and have a community." You need that ready kind of pipeline of organized people, who can take forward new sites.

Another example. At the moment, we're getting some pushback around the cost of our housing in the stuff that we're building in Lewisham. People are saying, is this really affordable? We've got what we think are very well-thought-out, unique affordability criteria that maps local incomes, projecting them in terms of what we call "genuinely affordable." But if that doesn't resonate with people's gut—if people who are going out 40 hours a week, working damn hard, and come home and say, "I still can't afford this"—then you can have the cleverest formula you want, but it's not worth the paper it's written on.

GREG ROSENBERG: Right. Right.

DAVE SMITH: So you've got to have that gut check in there. That's why resident involvement is so important because, organizationally, what happens otherwise is that you get this mission drift.

What some of the housing associations in the UK—not all, but some—can be accused of is being affordable housing providers who provide unaffordable housing. Organizationally, they have got to that place because of decreased resident involvement and a total reliance on professional boards, market conditions, and government grants. Largely, they build homes according to how much the government will give them in terms of grants to build them. That's how they come up with ideas like "80% of the market rate is affordable." What they mean is, "This is the rate we can now afford to build them at." But that is fundamentally different.

Unless you've got some check on that, unless you've got people saying, "No, it's fucking not affordable," then you just go, "Oh, okay, well that makes sense. That's what we can afford to pay for the land, and that's what we can afford to build, and that's how much it needs to cost. So, yeah."

Benefits for residents who get involved in the London CLT

GREG ROSENBERG: Let me ask you this. Say I'm one of the lucky people who gets to purchase a home from the London CLT. I have this guaranteed place to stay that's affordable to me. What's in it for me, as a resident, to continue to be involved in these community engagement, community organizing efforts? I've gotten what I want. What motivates people to continue to be involved?

DAVE SMITH: Well, Razia hasn't got a home yet, and she's still involved [laughs].

RAZIA KHANOM: [laughs]. I've been involved for a number of years.

There is some research that says why retail therapy is considered therapy. It is a momentary high. You know, serotonin levels, dopamine levels, all rising. But it wasn't sustained. You can't sustain it. The research then went on to show that giving to others, when others benefit without you actually having to spend any cash or gifts, kept that high for longer. So one could argue that there's a scientific reason why getting involved in these projects, continuously giving back to others, is actually good for your own mental wellbeing.

Coming back to myself and to why I'm involved. I was employed by a housing association over a decade ago. That's when I found out that there's a full-blown housing crisis and saw how organizations that are registered social landlords were part of the problem. Those affordable housing, shared ownership schemes, and all these other schemes, were touted as ways to tackle the housing crisis. But people realized that we still can't afford these places. And there is no genuine ownership to say that something is mine and take pride in it. There was still that weight hanging over your head. There's still somebody else that holds the cards, being able to tell me what to do.

I saw some policies being enacted—not just by social landlords, but by government as well—that caused housing insecurity. And it really broke me. Emotionally, it was really tough for me. I went on a bit of a journey. I said I'd never want to go into that industry again, or into that sector ever again.

Years later, we had London Citizens knocking on the door. I was really skeptical, because I've seen all these lovely luxury apartments coming up. It was called "affordable housing," but 80% of the people in the community still cannot afford this. Planning permission is based on, you know, one-third is going to be affordable housing. But by the time the houses are ready for people to move in they are told, "Sorry, our budget didn't allow for that." So that 30% is now turned into 5%. They say, "It's going to have to do, because we are not going to take those losses on our balance sheet."

So I was extremely skeptical. I became one of those that got caught in the need for secure, affordable housing. I still am. That was the initial reason why I turned up at the meeting. But I don't do this for me anymore. I find it hugely exhilarating that I am in this whole drive to provide not only affordable housing for people, but to allow the community to stay together. Families won't have to travel hours and hours or see each other at Christmas and Easter. There's still that connection, that support network in place when you desperately need them. We saw what COVID did when we couldn't visit family members.

That, for me, is my driving factor. It's not just one person I'm making a difference for; it could be a whole community, a small community. There could be maybe 100 people there. Their children then go on to benefiting from secure housing for the next generation. You know that you've created this chain of events. Long after our bones are turned into dust, people are still going to be benefiting.

That knowledge is what feeds me. I've had many late nights. We've had marathon board meetings. We've had very difficult board conversations. We've had very confrontational meetings with key partners. What keeps me going is I know that we're making a difference. We've got people in St. Clements. We're going to have people moving into Citizen's House. And by hook or by crook, we're going to make Christ Church Road happen.

I got involved in our Christ Church Road project because I live opposite it. I've seen this derelict land for 16 years, nothing being built there. I've challenged myself that we're going to make something happen there. I'm still continuing because I know somebody's going to benefit. Those people will appreciate it. Those are the ones we want to keep involved. But it will also inspire other people.

There is not a single person who learns about these London CLT projects and thinks it's a bad idea. Everybody wonders why we don't have more of this. We've had interviews with potential residents. Everybody wants to get involved. They're surprised this thing is not being supported by government on a larger scale. The support's there in the community. There's lots of people out there like me, doing the same thing, in our steering groups and in the wider community.

DAVE SMITH: I'm not even going to try and top that as an answer. It was spot on, wasn't it? I couldn't agree more with what Razia said. The only thing I'd add, I suppose, is that London CLT is very sincere about the fact that we don't just build houses. Looking at our tagline, we talk about homes and neighborhoods. What we're building, therefore, is not a static thing; it's not a thing that finishes. That's what other developers do: they come and build a building and then they go away because it's ended. But we're not in the business of building buildings like that. We're a business of building homes and continually thriving communities. If you're buying into that, if that's what you're purchasing, then why would you want to stop being a part of it once you've moved in?

Putting some fun into community work

GREG ROSENBERG: Razia, you were talking about the short-term high from retail therapy and then the crash. But there's this ongoing buzz from being involved in community organizing. Usually, when we talk about community organizing, we don't talk in terms of it being fun. Mostly we talk about it being hard. We're grinding. It's a battle. My sense, however, is that London CLT does a pretty good job of putting fun into its community engagement work. In my experience, if it's all work and no fun, people burn out, right? Do you have any thoughts about that?

RAZIA KHANOM: It is really hard. It is a grind. It is really challenging. It is really difficult. I bang my head against the proverbial wall many-a-day. This is why community matters. I might be tired today, but I've got this army behind me that has stepped up while I take a step back, taking a breather to recover, and then carry on.

That's what it's about. The end goal is our target. We're in it for the long game. Like Dave said earlier, once you accept that the work will never just be finished, once you make your peace with that, you'll understand that we're in it for the long run. It's like a relay race. I've got my baton for this leg. That's when I'm going to run my fastest and hardest to get the baton across. Then I'm done. At some points, my legs will be burning. Other points, you know, they'll be relaxing. It's part of that journey.

Is it fun? It depends on where you get your kicks. Certainly there are times where I take a step back and I am incredibly proud of myself for the journey that I've come along. I was a shadow of who I used to be. I've rediscovered that. And more crucially, interestingly enough, I see the impact that my work has on my children. Well, it's that cycle that continues. Is it fun? I don't know. Is it enjoyable? Absolutely, yes.

DAVE SMITH: As the first community organizer for London CLT, I'm really delighted to hear that as an observation. I think, "Poor old Razia. She is now Vice Chair of a multi-million-pound organization, with all the responsibility that brings." So I think "She's probably having the least fun of anybody!"

But I'd like to think that actually we do quite a good job, certainly at the entry level to the organization, of engaging people in a way that is quite good fun, with the music and the talks that we used to do—one of which you gave, Greg—and stuff like that. As an organizing tactic, you have to be conscious of things like that.

Two things we did quite well. One is tell people a story that they could involve themselves in, that had a narrative that they were a part of. And the second thing was to make it fun along the way.

You need some humility here. There's a lot of good causes in the world. Cancer is important. Ukraine is important. Africa. Yemen. Race. Child poverty. There's lots of important stuff out there—arguably much more important than ours. So you've got to make it worth people's time to get involved.

It's an organizing mantra, isn't it, that mutual self-interest is not a bad thing necessarily. If part of that self-interest is bringing people into a relationship with each other, then having a good time is part of it. I don't think that's bad. It's a marketplace of ideas and causes. We're trying to rally as many people as we can around ours.

So I'm pleased that there's a perception that sometimes we have some fun, even if Razia and I don't always get to witness it!

GREG ROSENBERG: Your Shuffle Festival, that was such a brilliant idea. It was a way to kind of activate a site before development happened, to start bringing people together. That's such a nice story. It's something that other CLTs don't think to do in that kind of a way. I saw that as really benefiting your development work at St Clements.

DAVE SMITH: So that scared the life out of me, the Shuffle Film Festival!

GREG ROSENBERG: [laughs].

DAVE SMITH: I've never done anything as hard in my entire life. The Shuffle Film Festival never would have happened without Kate McTiernan and Lizzy Daish (and many others, Jess, Miranda... too). But Kate and Lizzy were the two board members who drove it forward. We need their names in print.

There's a really important point there about diversity on boards. I don't think they were people who traditional organizations would look to appoint on their boards. They brought an enthusiasm and a creativity and ability to do that in a way that none of us ever could. I remember Callum Green who had just started at London CLT and went on to work as Executive Director, saying to me, "Dave, if it had just been me and you, it would have been like, you know, when you've got like a projector and a little pull-up rubbish screen and a few chairs laid out." [Laughs].

Instead, it was really special. They assembled a wonderful team around them. And all the credit for it has to go to Lizzy and to Kate and those who worked with them for building it, for pushing it through, for how it looked, for making it happen. It was transformative, I think, in terms of the breadth of people that it engaged.

GREG ROSENBERG: Well, I think we limit ourselves into what community land trusts can do, particularly culturally, right? That was such a huge cultural benefit to the community to do that. You're doing housing, but I see that kind of thing as being just as important when it comes to community building.

DAVE SMITH: Yeah.

Giving voice to the "community"

GREG ROSENBERG: Speaking of community, we throw that word around a lot without really defining what we mean by that, right? At this point, you are a city-wide CLT in one of the largest cities in the world. When you talk about serving the community, how do you define "community"? Is it multiple communities, or do you have a narrative that encompasses everybody? What do you think?

DAVE SMITH: Well, don't take this wrong, Greg, it's not aimed at you. But I think it's a really boring (and often unnecessary) question that we get asked all the time. And my answer to it is: we define community by the people who put themselves forward, who self-nominate and want to be involved with it, those who show up and show they care; those who step up and say, "I want to be a part of this community thing that's going on here."

As professional organizers, you also need to make sure, if that's your approach, that you're ensuring there's no barriers to access to people.

GREG ROSENBERG: Right.

DAVE SMITH: When we were doing the St Clements project, asking people to come along to a community planning event in a Methodist church isn't as open, appealing, or accessible to all of the community as it could be. So we did things like make sure that we ran one in the East London mosque as well, and the school opposite, to make it as available as possible.

But this idea of who's in the community, who's out of the community, what are the geographical boundaries of the community? To me, that just speaks to a different type of politics. It's a state-based politics, with its kind of universal egalitarianism. It ends up being nothing to anybody in its attempt to be all things to all people, with its rules and definitions and structures and subcommittees and processes.

Sorry, that probably wasn't the answer you were hoping for. I'm just kind of bored of it as a question. Because it has been used to try and box us in and to delegitimize us in the past. But, Razia, I don't know what you think about that?

RAZIA KHANOM: Dave's been doing this much longer than I, so I can appreciate his viewpoint of it being a little bit boring. But I find it quite an interesting question.

My answer changes, depending on who's asking it. Somebody from our local community group, somebody who's looking to support us, would never ask that question. As a group of people who have come together, if they're campaigning for housing, they've basically gotten fed up with people who they've appointed to do the job and are not doing the job. Or to put it quite frankly, they have utterly failed at what they've been elected to do.

Who is this community? For me, it's a group of people that have come together, who are looking to take affirmative action. It shouldn't be necessary, which is the key thing here. That community can morph into whether it's needed locally or needed in London.

A couple of weeks ago, because I've gotten involved with London CLT and the International CLT Festival, I spoke with Theresa Williamson for the Favela CLT Network. That is also part of my community now. It's a movement that we've all started. Attending that discussion with Brazil left me feeling renewed in my energies. That's what we do in communities. We help each other. We support each other. And we're also inspiring each other.

So what is a community? It's what you want it to mean. Dave's right, we don't need to be asking that question anymore. What we need to be asking is, "Why are these people shouting for something? Why? Where has it gone wrong?" Let's sort that out. Then we don't have to worry about what is community.

DAVE SMITH: Razia's was a far more eloquent way of saying what I was trying to say!

RAZIA KHANOM: [laughs].

GREG ROSENBERG: Dave, you talked about meeting people in places where they're comfortable, and then removing barriers to people getting involved. Then, Razia, there was something that you said during one of our webinars last year, that activism could sometimes be the privilege of those who are a little well off. If you're wanting to represent all the voices in the community, how can you do it in a way that doesn't skew it towards folks who are in a better position to take the time to participate?

RAZIA KHANOM: This is where the work of London CLT, and actually even more the work London Citizens, is exceptional. Those who have the time, the privilege of time can work on behalf of others. London Citizens, the campaigning organization, comes in to do the grassroots work, making contact with people that perhaps don't have that availability of time. How well they do that job goes on to determine the success, which is: how do you project those voices and accurately reflect that and bring it back to more active campaigning?

So, to give you an example. Once upon a time, I may not have had the time to do a lot of the work I've done. What the pandemic did was to allow a lot of people who may have been stuck at home, no childcare, or perhaps working unsociable hours. We're all on zoom, we're able to have these conversations, so it becomes inclusive there. London Citizens are doing a social mobility campaign with my daughter's school, with a group of people that, generally, are extremely marginalized. It took one leader within that organization to approach London Citizens and say, "We need a campaign that looks at social mobility and how our community's voices can be heard. We can't tell you what their needs are. Speak to the community. We'll create the space so you can hear them directly."

London Citizens swooped in to hear straight from the horse's mouth what's going on. They've got the experience, they've got the skillset, but they are not diluting the voices of those who may not have the time. It is this type of partnership that allows us to accurately relay those voices.

I can bring this back to what London CLT has done for me. I would ordinarily not have been on a board. I've never been on a board before. I've never been in a position to have my voice heard before. But London CLT—and the way it operates in terms of its democratic organization—ensures that the community is part of the voices being heard. They are part of the high-stakes decision-making platforms as well, transporting those voices, making sure that those voices are not diluted and not forgotten.

So far, I think we're doing quite a good job. Otherwise, I wouldn't be here [laughs].

DAVE SMITH: The only thing I'd add is that we're a business as well. London CLT is a business. We have to get hold of land and build homes and sell them to survive. And we have a consumer base, which is the people we're trying to serve. So there's no world in which all we can be are well-meaning, middle class campaigners doing it out of the goodness of our hearts. We have a consumer base who is part of the organization as well, who is buying the product because it makes financial sense according to their self-interest.

The proof is in the fact that, when we knock these homes up, people line up round the block to buy them off us. It's an essential part of the business model. You know, there's a world in which some organizations can survive by having wealthy middle-class people writing letters or whatever. That is possible within their business model. The London CLT can't operate without people who aren't deeply self-interested in getting an affordable home.

Balancing the roles of organizer and developer

GREG ROSENBERG: That leads me to something that I've wrestled with myself. I've done work as an organizer and I've done work as a housing developer. To me, some overlapping skills are required for both, but they're very different mindsets. To me, they're radically different. When I'm in developer mode, I'm an autocrat, I want to hit deadlines. Group participation, group decision-making is an annoyance, right? It's like, is this going to improve the quality of the decision? If not, then why are we doing this, right?

In an organizer mode, I'm all about process, group building, leadership development, all that stuff. I can't do them both at the same time and do either one justice.

Now, as an organization, you're doing both, right? You're the developer and you're the organizer. How are you managing those somewhat conflicting roles, and maintaining integrity in both areas?

DAVE SMITH: We struggle too. I think it's a really fair question. I think of the four Executive Directors that we've had at London CLT, including me, and nobody has embodied both of those roles evenly or perfectly, by any means. That's no critique of colleagues we've had who came after me, all of whom have done and are doing a very capable job. But I think you're right, they're inherently two different things.

A really practical organizational answer to your question is that we're starting to realize that we need different staff with different skills. It's about an organizational balance, rather than trying to have one person who can do all of those things.

Hannah Emery Wright, who has worked for London CLT for a long time, does a really good job of trying to mix those skills. She brings with her a lot of the community side of it. Whereas in Oliver Bulleid, our current ED, we've got somebody who is an architect by profession. He's more familiar with the development side of it. They're both very interested in and very capable at the other sides of the business, but I think organizationally we've probably decided that we are unlikely to ever get one person who embodies all of those kinds of things. So, at a staff level, as long as they're aware and appreciative of the other side of the coin, that's quite important.

I don't think there's ever a business or a system where autocracy doesn't move things forward quicker. But you've got to ask yourselves about what it is, ultimately, that you value coming out the end of it. We could probably knock our houses up cheaper and quicker if we didn't involve people in the process. Everything has got a cost-benefit to it. We put huge weight on the participation, the quality of it, and the quality building aspect of it as well.

RAZIA KHANOM: A saying comes to mind, "Jack of all trades, master of none." It's a very unreasonable expectation to have one person embody everything. I don't think we, or anybody, would be as successful in achieving their goals if we were to do that. It's quite interesting that Dave makes mention of our current CEO, and Hannah, our campaigns manager. The way you could view it is they're counterbalances for each other.

GREG ROSENBERG: Right.

RAZIA KHANOM: When we do what we're particularly good at, something we're particularly skilled at, we thrive; we achieve the best results. To ask somebody to come out of that zone is doing them—and the organization—a disservice. How we recruit is very important. Our board reflects that ethos as well. We have those who will accept risk everywhere. There are others who are looking at making sure that things are developed well. Then there are others, like myself, who will say, "Whoa horsey, take a step back in getting there. Hold on, we've still got some baggage. We've got a wagon behind us. We need to bring along our communities."

It's not to say that one way is correct and the other is incorrect. It's how you are ensuring that your organizational ethos and your values continue, through development, to serve those communities. I would say, yes, it is a challenge. Sometimes when I come into a board meeting, I have to take off my finance hat and remember that I'm here to represent communities and what communities would want. That's the hat I have to wear; that's why I'm here; and that's what will serve the organization best.

It's good to have that conflict within the board, because it means we're having those critical conversations to make sure that not only are we developing, but that we're staying true to our ethos. We're being innovative and creating those communities. I think, so far, we're quite good at that.

Resolving conflicts

GREG ROSENBERG: It's interesting that you mention the term "conflict." John Davis often talks about the rationale behind the tripartite board. He says, "We always anticipated there would be a conflict of interests. We set it up in way so people would have to work things out with each other. It doesn't mean that a CLT is somehow failing if there's conflict among board members. If they're unable to resolve it, that's a problem. But there should be some disagreement, some conflict, because people's self-interest will vary, sometimes quite strongly."

So I was wondering, were there issues or projects where the board struggled with each other to find their way through that?

RAZIA KHANOM: We have had some conflict within the board. A number of elements came into play. Speaking from my personal perspective on this, I came at it through the lens that we are here to represent our membership and our communities, to deliver for those. There were some decisions where I went against my own thought process, because you have to make that decision.

I know that what I would like to do may not be that which needs to be done. There are situations where, I think, Dave and I have both reluctantly made decisions, because we knew that it was in the best interest of the of the organization. In an ideal situation, we would never have wanted to be in that position.

But there's also been unity within that conflict, despite our personal choices and wants and needs. I think that highlights the need to overcome one's own ego in order to make sure that the community is preserved, the projects are preserved, and the work can continue.

DAVE SMITH: London CLT is not unique, but all British CLTs don't follow the "classic" tripartite CLT model as closely as we do. There's a lot of variation around it.

London CLT very consciously chose to adopt that, and we stick to it still. But it's a very American model. John Davis talks brilliantly about the international influences on the CLT model. But it's John Locke, isn't it? It's republicanism, separation of powers, Federalist Papers stuff. It's a balance of powers among different branches. And it works well within that history and within that context. But within a British governing context, we're far more used to working via consensus in a kind of an unconstituted sense. So perhaps we don't take to it as naturally or as readily, just at a cultural level.

The other part I'd add is that we're changing the board slightly at the moment to make sure that the non-resident community aspect of the board represents what we call "community steering groups." These are people who are working in a local area, around a particular site. They're kind of a hyper-local group, representing the next site that London CLT develops.

Previously, what we've had are residents on the board, and they're quite clear and strong about what they want and what their priorities are. Then there's the kind of municipal board representatives who look out for the interest of the organization and the whole city.

Subsequently, we got to a situation where we've had a few sites come forward, where basically people are campaigning locally for it. They say, "We want to do this." And the board has said, "We want to do that as well, but that would bankrupt the organization [laughs]. We can't build them at a price that you think is affordable in that location, despite the fact it's where you are and where you care about it."

That has led to situations where there has been a too-ready disconnect between the people on the ground and the London CLT board. Rather than them seeing the board as an extension of the campaign groups, they've seen the board as people who are trying to put roadblocks in the way, or people not on the same page as them.

In my mind at least, it was helpful for us to talk through where there was some kind of conflict. I think the tripartite system probably does still work, but I think you've got to be really sure that people are aware of who they're supposed to be representing in those different three segments, in order to balance the powers properly.

GREG ROSENBERG: Yes. I also would say, in an American context, that I would guess the vast majority of decisions made by CLT boards are by consensus, even though consensus is not required.

Expanding the CLT's service area

GREG ROSENBERG: As you were talking about the community steering groups, it got me wondering about the leap from being the East London CLT to being the London CLT. I'm guessing maybe the community steering groups were one of the things that you started working with as you expanded city-wide. Is that true? I'm really interested in how you made that leap from serving just one part of the city to serving the entire city.

DAVE SMITH: It was on the back of people like Razia, who were making such a strong case for the London CLT elsewhere. I'll let her talk to it because she, far more than me, was kind of responsible for this leap.

RAZIA KHANOM: Thank you, Dave. But it would be unfair for me to take the entire credit. Actually, it's one of the things that inspired me to continue to be involved, not only out of a sense of camaraderie, but actually a sense of accountability. Our community steering group in Christ Church Road, in southwest London, was born out of two young lads, 17 years old I think they were at the time. They were really angry with the housing situation here. "Where we live, where we were born, where our parents were born, where our grandparents were born is becoming so gentrified. After we graduate from university or college, we will not be able to afford to live here. There will come a situation where I will have to hop onto two or three trains just to visit my mother's grave."

These types of stories really give you a full perspective of why these projects are needed. When I went to that first steering group meeting, I wasn't sure what to expect. I heard those stories and I realized that my parent's generation hadn't done enough to make sure that the future's secure for the next generation. They'll finish higher education with a mountain of debt on their heads, with no kind of prospect of being able to live a family life. I mean, who wants to go on to meet the love of their lives, go on and get your pet dog, or go on to have children when you've already got this weight on your head?

Just hearing those stories made me realize how important it is to do this. I felt I was accountable, to make sure that I did my bit to be part of that campaign to make it happen. There were times when we were having conversations with a steering group and I was thinking perhaps this project is unviable. What do we do?

Feeding off each other's energies we realized that, "No, we're not going to accept this. We're not going to go down without the fight." And our tagline became, "We're going to throw everything and the kitchen sink at this, and fight that fight, and burn everything down, and leave. Then we'll know that we've given it everything we had."

Here we are, about a year-and-a-half later. We're still here, and that feeds into why we continue. It's not just me. It's these two young lads, growing into fine young men. We've got my co-chair—although he's no longer a co-chair. He's put the reins down. But it's this fluidity that happens within the community. We drive each other in doing that. And personal stories inspire each other. When we're speaking about these things in the local community, other people are coming forward with their needs as to why they need housing. It just feeds into that whole energy and that whole drive.

It's our community driving it. We've had enough. And it's not just here in South London. I've spoken to Bernie. (Dave, you know Bernie, she's been doing this work for probably longer than I've been alive.) They don't give up. She's been doing it for decades [laughs]. There are people like that who refuse to take no for an answer. It's those people who come forward, who we get together with and form that wall.

DAVE SMITH: I think the expansion from the East London CLT to the London CLT was a reaction to circumstance, as well as a strategic growth decision. I think we always would have said we wanted to do that. But because of the close relationship with the London Citizens network, other people heard about the success with St Clements in Mile End. And then there were campaigns like Razia's and the other one that we should definitely mention, Brasted Close in Lewisham. The work of two phenomenal leaders, a teacher called Janet Emmanuel and Nano McCaughan, just ran such a wonderful campaign. They moved it forward and got some land. London CLT couldn't walk away from it.

You can have a position where you're ready to take on another site in South London. You say to yourself, "Okay, if we're going to do that, we need a governance structure which reflects and represents people from every part of the city." So that was kind of how it came about.

GREG ROSENBERG: Opportunistic, not strategic. It's nice.

DAVE SMITH: I've been called worse. Yeah, I'll go along with that. Yeah [laughs].

GREG ROSENBERG: Opportunistic. I don't see that as a bad word.

New tools for organizing after the pandemic

GREG ROSENBERG: I have one last question. This is kind of the technology nerd in me. This pandemic has brought us entirely new tools for engaging folks. Organizers have a different tool belt than they had five years ago. Once life returns to a sense of normalcy (although it may never return to where it was before), what are tools that you utilized in the pandemic that you would see as valuable going forward? Is there technology that's been used during the pandemic that has actually increased opportunities for participation?

RAZIA KHANOM: I think for me, speaking from my own experience, there are a lot of events like this that I normally wouldn't have been able to take part in, because I don't have adequate childcare in place. Right now, I'm in this room and I can hear the children making a racket over there. But I don't have to rely on external care which is something that is really hard to come by for me. There are people I know that perhaps have larger social anxieties. They can remain a little more conspicuous when they're online. Traveling to and from events can elongate the whole process in terms of the time required. Right now, from my living room, I can log on in five minutes, rather than having an hour-and-a-half commute to different meetings across London.

So, for a lot of people, it's allowed them to partake in events that they probably normally wouldn't have given the time commitment that is needed. That's something I would still like to see us continue to utilize. I think that it is going to be part of our new normal, not just in-person meetings. Strategically, we'll be able to harness the voices of those who normally wouldn't have been able to participate.

It's definitely a tool that we've utilized. Just to give you an example, we had an ideas workshop for our steering committee. We had to cancel this in-person event because the Omicron variant suddenly appeared. But we still managed to get over 45 people at our online consultation. We left with the architects telling us, "This is actually amazing because during in-person events we were lucky if we got 15–20 people." So we were able to reach out to more people. And using things like Facebook, we're able to target certain geographical locations in order to publicize our events. It certainly has its uses.

But in-person events also have their uses in terms of the kind of energies that you get off each other. The AGM that we had in 2020 was amazing, seeing residents and seeing children coming in and presenting their story. It's good to be in each other's company and energy. So they both serve their purposes.

GREG ROSENBERG: Dave, any thoughts?

DAVE SMITH: I agree with Razia, as I often do. Razia's perspective, as a resident and mother, all of those things, is the most important one. The only thing I could add to that, I suppose, is from an organizer's perspective. What the return to the world, as we are trying to do, has done post-pandemic, is to make you really think about whether or not a meeting needs to be in-person or online. Before, the default was in-person, right? There's no replacement if you're trying to build relationships. There's no replacement for in-person.

But like you said earlier, when we were talking about the role of the CLT, it straddles both the relational organizing work and the bureaucratic getting-houses-built work. It forces you to bring into context each decision, each meeting you have. What is the purpose of this? Where am I trying to go with it? You then make a decision about the nature of the meeting, on the back of that. I think it's quite interesting that it forces you to address the chief purpose of the meeting.

The online Annual General Meeting we did was wonderful, but we would never do that out of choice because the purpose of the AGM is relational. But if I'm meeting with an architect, as we used to do for St Clements, to talk about the bloody depth of window recesses or whatever, why am I traveling there for an hour on the train both ways? I can do that bureaucratic meeting via zoom.

So the ability to do meetings online has, I think, brought the teaching about the difference between bureaucratic and relational meetings into sharper focus.

GREG ROSENBERG: Interesting. I must say I enjoyed the band that you had for your last AGM.

DAVE SMITH: They were good, weren't they?

GREG ROSENBERG: It was just great. They rocked out so hard!

DAVE SMITH: They were the most polite young rock band I've ever met. I kind of got up, and I was going to let them finish their song before we started, and they kind of stopped mid-song. And I said, "No, you can finish; you can finish your song" [laughs].

GREG ROSENBERG: [laughs].

DAVE SMITH: I always say, "Punk is not dead. It's just more polite than it used to be."

Building trust

GREG ROSENBERG: Well, that's it for my questions. Do you have had any other things that you want to mention before we end this? Don't feel obligated, but if there's something we didn't cover that you really wished to touch on, I want to give you a chance to do that.

RAZIA KHANOM: I did, actually. It was something that you picked up on, something that I said in a previous meeting about trust-building.

GREG ROSENBERG: Right.

RAZIA KHANOM: I made a conscious decision to speak about that because it's not only a service that I'm doing for myself in terms of overcoming my own personal traumas, a voice that I wished I had when I was much younger. A lot of self-reflection has led to this process. It came out of what has become quite a hostile environment in the UK in terms of migrants, in terms of what is considered ethnic minority communities.

I've experienced a lot of hostility because of the way I look. It confused me a lot, because I was born here. I have my children. Their first language is English. Although I'm bilingual, it's quite difficult, for they identify as British children. They've had to witness their mother being verbally abused because somebody thinks that I don't belong here.

It led me on a journey of trying to understand why I went into my shell. And trying to understand this idea that, somehow, "Ethnic minorities, when they come here, they don't integrate. Why don't they integrate? They don't accept us." It led me to look back and speak with my mother. Suddenly it became clear as day. When she first came to this country, they came here as economic migrants. It was post-partition in India and the post-independence war in Bangladesh, which led to famine. They came over here, essentially, because at that point in time my father was still a British citizen. But when they came here it was extremely hostile, so hostile that they feared for their lives to go out on their own.

They had to form communities to survive. Coming back to that question of communities, we live in communities for our survival. I'll remind you of what I was saying about cavemen: it's essential to our survival. They came here with hopes and dreams and they were rejected. They were abused. They were told they don't belong here. So they closed off into their own communities.

We have come a long way in terms of racial awareness, in terms of diversity, in terms of inclusion. But those traumas are still there. My mother will not forget being attacked. My mother will not forget being abused. And for the first time in recent years, I've experienced that too. The shock that descended on me; it was just entire shock. What do you do? Do you respond? How do you then explain this to your children? Your children are witnesses to this.

One of the things that I would get from some of my Asian community and, locally, from my Muslim community, is how do you do your work without your identity being threatened? Which is what large groups of the Asian community, South Asian communities, and Muslim communities have faced. We've seen that with how migrants or refugees that arrive here, the kind of treatment they get and how the media will treat them.

Interestingly, when London Citizens was doing work in terms of social mobility and created that safe space, they were astounded. One of the organizers said, "I don't understand. We've been asked to investigate why your school has had such a large uptake on the social mobility campaigns and the mental wellbeing campaigns, because we haven't seen that rate of uptake anywhere else."

Coming back to trust-building, it's not that these communities don't want to be involved. They came with bright-eyed, bushy-tailed hopes and dreams. And they were shot down. So now we have to undo some of that from the past, to show everybody these doors are actually open for you. Come and give us what you have.

Then you see those groups of people coming in and taking full ownership. So much so that when we had our Lambeth delegates assembly, I thought housing was going to make the top of the list easily until these groups came in and just took over and said, "Sorry, we've got our safe space. We've had enough. We want social mobility high up on the agenda now. And that came in at second place. And housing went from one to three.

London Citizens or Lambeth citizen campaigners are doing the work to show these communities that we're actually making progress here. You are part of the community. We want to hear what you have to say, so that your communities can address social mobility, and social mobility can improve.

It's amazing the kind of impact that can have, the input they can have, and what those communities create alone or together for survival. We do ourselves such a disservice when we don't tap into that energy because that community can be bigger, it can be stronger, and you, as a wider community, can benefit from that.

I talk on it, because some people don't get involved because there are traumas involved. That's something that we as campaigners, those with the privilege of being able to present their voices, need to find ways to harness that energy they have. It's something that I feel I have full remit of, within London CLT.

Coming back to accountability and readdressing going into a shell myself, I now have the platform. I now have the choice. Do I just benefit myself and this little campaign, or do we help each other to come up together?

That's why I say when their voices are not being heard, "Do not assume that they are silent." It's like a tree falling in a forest. Is it making a sound or not? That's what we have to take into account.

GREG ROSENBERG: What a wonderful way to end this remarkable conversation. Thank you.

DAVE SMITH: Thank you, Greg, for investing the time and the preparation. Nobody knows us better than you. You're a valued supporter and friend of London CLT. The organization thinks of you very fondly, so thank you for the time you've put into the conversation this afternoon.

GREG ROSENBERG: Well, I am president of the Wisconsin chapter of the London CLT Fan Club.

DAVE SMITH: [laughs]. Good, good, good!

RAZIA KHANOM: [laughs]. Thank you, Greg. I really appreciate that. And you, Dave, as always.

GREG ROSENBERG: Thank you so much, to both of you.

5.

A Conversation with Geert De Pauw, Brussels Community Land Trust

Hosted by Dave Smith
April 21, 2022

DAVE SMITH: Welcome Geert, and thanks so much for doing this. Can I start by saying what a huge fan I've been of your work, for a long, long time? We first met in 2009, I think, during the trip to the Champlain Housing Trust, when they won the World Habitat Award. It's been a real pleasure to watch the Brussels CLT grow from that point.

I've got a lot of questions in front of me. But I wanted to start by getting a bit of an idea about you. I think, because of your modesty, you are often the untold part of the Brussels CLT story. So please give me a few minutes on how you got involved in this, how you came to it.

GEERT DE PAUW: I was a community worker in a neighborhood in Brussels called Molenbeek, working in a community center called Bonnevie. We were working with low-income families, mainly on housing issues. We did a lot of things like giving them advice on how to refurbish their homes, but also more action-oriented stuff. We had an action group on housing rights with people from the neighborhoods.

Brussels is a very rich city, but also a city with a lot of people on low incomes and big inequality. It has very little social housing, but for a long time, until 15 or 20 years ago, Brussels was reasonably affordable. The market could supply affordable housing for low-income people. That changed after 2000 when housing prices started to rise.

One of the groups we were working with were migrant people with large families. The main housing policies in Belgium are meant to help people become homeowners, and a lot of migrant families were able to buy their own home, mostly in low-quality houses. But that became more and more challenging or impossible as housing prices were rising.

So we started thinking about other possibilities for developing affordable housing for these families. We were interested in community-led approaches, something which we didn't find any examples of in Belgium at that point. I think we were really the first ones who were working on housing issues with this kind of approach.

Together with CIRE, an association working with migrants and refugees, and with the help of a social housing organization called Fonds du Logement, we managed to develop a community-led housing project called l'Espoir. It is a building of 14 flats for low-income families who were at the center of planning this project. They played a very important role in the design, but also in the campaigning to make it possible, to find the funding, to find the land, et cetera.

This project was delivered some 13 years ago now, and was very successful. We really learned by doing, but we also saw that this community-led approach had a lot of added value compared to other forms of affordable housing.

DAVE SMITH: That's brilliant. I've been there and seen it. It's fantastic. Were you working for the government at that point, before you moved to the Brussels CLT?

GEERT DE PAUW: No, personally I was active in different housing rights movements in Brussels but, professionally, I was working for an NGO, a community center.

DAVE SMITH: Perhaps we'll come back to that later on because I think the contrast is interesting between CLTs which are established by the State and CLTs which are established outside of the State. Were you born in Brussels? Did you grow up in Brussels?

GEERT DE PAUW: No, I don't live in Brussels, even now. I live on the periphery of Brussels. I grew up not so far from where I live now.

DAVE SMITH: Has that been interesting for you to work in a community that you don't live in? Do you find that beneficial or more difficult?

GEERT DE PAUW: I think I can say that I managed to do my job without living in the community. I can't say if it would've been better or easier. I don't know.

Is community involvement the "right" thing to do?

DAVE SMITH: You were a panelist for both of last year's webinars that considered the meaning and the importance of community and community organizing in the CLT movement. Today we're going to delve more deeply into those topics and give you a chance to expand on your earlier remarks.

Let's start with the rationale for involving residents in planning and managing the multi-unit housing being developed by CLT Brussels. Why does CLT Brussels involve so many people? More generally, why do you think community involvement is the "right" thing to do?

GEERT DE PAUW: Well [laughing], that's a very large question. As I said before, in our earlier project, we learned that community involvement is beneficial for many reasons.

We should make a distinction between campaigning to get the government to support a community's interest, and the CLT promoting community involvement in governing the CLT and in developing housing. These are three different things, I think, although some of the arguments are similar for all three.

In terms of campaigning on behalf the community's interest, we started to understand how the community land trust model could be something important for the Brussels region. It was important for us, first of all, to involve people with housing needs in our work. We had to understand if, for them, it was really such a good idea. We had to check to see if what we saw as a good idea was also something that was supported by those we wanted to do it for. In terms of campaigning, rather than go to see government officials with people who professionally think that something would be a good idea, it makes a huge difference if you go to government officials with people who say, "Yes, we need this. Yes, we want this. Yes, we want to be involved in this."

That really changed everything. Otherwise, we never would have been listened to. So that's the campaigning part: both checking with different stakeholders who you could call the beneficiaries of future housing and creating the leverage to convince government officials.

Then, we had to start thinking through what exactly we want here in Brussels and what form do we want to give to this community land trust. When it came to developing the governance part of the community land trust, this was a very important battle for us. In Brussels, and in most cities, you can come together with five people and create a CLT. It is not so very difficult. But, of course, when you want to develop affordable housing for low-income families with this community land trust, you need public money to make that possible. We got interest from the government and we started negotiating with them over the terms on which we could get public money for our operation.

We were negotiating with the intention of giving a lot of power to residents and to other neighbors. But it took a lot of time to convince government officials of this, because they wanted control over the operation they would fund.

But for us, it was really one of the important issues. Why? Because we think that better decisions will be made when all the stakeholders are involved in an equal way. Also, we really think there is a lot of potential among people who are considered to be a population that has to be helped or, even worse, who are seen as people who are a source of problems. But we think there is a lot of unused potential there. Having them in the governance system of the organization is bringing a lot of important assets.

DAVE SMITH: I think it's a very nice way to think about it actually, those three different parts: the campaign for government support of the community land trust; the building of homes; and, then, the organizational management, the governance, the stewardship.

Is it a practical thing for you to involve residents in designing the houses before they're built and involving residents in the management of the housing after they're built? I know that CLTB does both. You don't just do that out of ideology. You do it because, practically, you think that it produces better places to live?

GEERT DE PAUW: Hmm. Well, I must say that over time, our practice has changed. Indeed, in the very beginning, we wanted to involve future residents from the very beginning in the design of the projects. We thought that it could be essential for having a better design. That is something we did for our first two projects. Later on, we tweaked it a bit. We discovered [laughing], that we were very new with all these things and very idealistic. We discovered that building processes can be very challenging, with difficulties that can add a lot of time. If you plan for a process of two years, but it actually takes five years, that can be too much for future residents.

So what we do now is to organize workshops at the beginning of projects where we ourselves are going to be the developer. We involve people who already live in our homes and other community members, but not necessarily those who will live in the new homes. The results of the earlier workshops then get integrated into the tenders for the architects. The chosen architect will then do all the procedures to get the building permits. Once we have the permits, which can sometimes take quite a lot of time, we'll allocate the homes.

Whereas, for our first couple of projects, we formed the group of future residents at the very beginning of the project, we now do that after having obtained the permits. We developed another way of working, therefore, where we can have the benefits of involving all these people in the design process, but without all the burdens of what we did before.

DAVE SMITH: So the community is really the client for the architect?

GEERT DE PAUW: Yeah, the community land trust, yes. Once we have the permits, then we bring together the group. We do the allocations and we have a group of future residents. Then it takes, let's say, two more years while the building is being constructed.

DAVE SMITH: You're allocating homes to future residents two years before the housing is built?

GEERT DE PAUW: Yeah. And during those two years, the future residents have a say in how the homes will be managed, what kind of activities we will develop there, what kind of relationship they will have with the neighborhood, et cetera.

It's also important to know that it's different in Brussels than in London, for instance. In London, the allocation procedure strongly focuses on connection with a local community. In Brussels it's not like that. We do our allocations of homes based on a waiting list where people can register from all over the Brussels region. Very often, they don't have any connection with the neighborhood where they are going to settle.

DAVE SMITH: One of the other differences is that we allocate at the end of it. We wouldn't be able to get people to wait for two years, because they have likely moved to something else in the meantime. It strikes me that what you are doing is creating a very intentional community, a group of people who very much want to be there, given their involvement for two years waiting to get a home?

GEERT DE PAUW: People are willing to invest so much time and wait so long because there are very few alternatives. Most of these people register for CLT housing mainly because they are looking for affordable housing. It's not because they want to live together with other families and do fancy things together. They are looking for affordable housing. Our housing projects are not really intentional communities when we start the process.

One of the focuses of our work before people move into their homes is to try to build a community out of that. That's the main community work we do now around our housing projects. It's very much linked to the fact that most of our housing projects are collective buildings, I mean multi-unit buildings. In Brussels, we cannot develop single-family homes. So a lot of the work we do is focused on creating a community that is able to manage this kind of project, to help people know their future neighbors, and to learn how to make collective decisions, et cetera.

DAVE SMITH: Do people ever move out of your houses, or do they tend to stay there pretty much forever?

GEERT DE PAUW: Well, it's a bit soon to say, because our first homes were delivered a little more than five years ago. Up to now, there have been only three families that moved. All of them moved to other CLT homes. They did so because their apartment didn't fit the family size anymore.

DAVE SMITH: I know that a big part for you, especially in your stewardship and governance, is involving people in the CLT who don't live in CLT homes. You have a broader membership?

GEERT DE PAUW: That's true. This broader membership comes from a lot of NGOs and community organizations who are really crucial to all of our work. All that we do is always with other partners. We never do something on our own. It's really very important for us to be able to work with people who know the local communities.

Other people living in Brussels who believe in what we do can also become members. We try to involve them too. I must say, however, that in the last couple of years this has not been something we have been investing a lot of time into. When we started, it was important, indeed, to bring together all kinds of civil society organizations and activists and people with housing needs to have the same message. Today, our priority is to support the communities living in our housing projects. I do regret a bit, though, that we have neglected this wider dimension in the last couple years. But you can't do everything [laughing]. So . . .

DAVE SMITH: Of course, it's the constant challenge of balancing different parts, isn't it? But when working with London CLT and then having worked with housing corporations in the UK, I've realized the importance of including people who don't live in the homes. Otherwise, organizations can become very insular and self-regarding and not look to build more.

GEERT DE PAUW: Hmm. Yeah.

The place of "community" in
Organismes de Foncier Solidaire

DAVE SMITH: I want to shift our conversation to another topic and talk about the French version of the CLT—the OFS. You are in Brussels. You are the CLT torch-carriers for Europe. I know that CLTs are starting to prosper in neighboring France. They do it somewhat differently, however. They take the land off the market using ground leases for their projects. And they're permanently preserving the affordability of whatever housing is developed on land that is owned by an OFS. These land trusts are doing really good work. But, in some ways, it's quite hard to call them community land trusts, isn't it?

I wonder if you could say a little bit about that. Do you think there are any advantages to the French model? Or are there disadvantages to the fact they don't embrace the "C" in CLT as readily as your CLT in Brussels?

GEERT DE PAUW: I think it's important to understand the French culture and the way that policy is made in France, which is much more top-down than in our country and in many other European countries. There's really this culture of Paris deciding.

That was how CLTs came about in France. It started with politicians passing legislation to make community land trusts possible—which has proven to be very successful. That is unusual, if you compare it to other countries, where it's often many years of developing CLT housing and campaigning before you manage to convince the authorities to recognize this system. It was the other way around in France. They did it that way mainly as a reaction to very unsustainable ways of helping people into homeownership. Classical homeownership programs have many disadvantages, which you know about. That was their main reason to opt for new legislation.

I think it is a very good question whether you can you call OFS a "community land trust." Indeed, not in all the cases, because community is a very important part of a CLT. But we know of city-led organizations and social housing organizations and old cooperatives that are taking the initiative to create an OFS that are really interested in the community approach. Some of them are really trying to see how community can be integrated into their model. But should you call it a CLT or not? That's a difficult strategic question.

DAVE SMITH: I actually think we can get too worried about definitions sometimes. Your point is a really good and important one. CLTs had to fit within the cultural framework of France and how municipalities work and how decisions are made. Everywhere is going to innovate and do things slightly differently.

I suppose the question is: What are the core bits? I suppose there has to be a degree of shared equity. And then community involvement. Can you envisage whether someday there will be greater community ownership in the French model than you see at the moment? Is that the way it could go?

GEERT DE PAUW: Oh, yeah, I think there's really an intention to do it that way in France. In this French system you also have another legal instrument for housing development that is, let's call it, "collaborative housing." It has other rules and other target groups. Some OFS leaders are looking for ways they could combine both models.

Audrey Linkenheld, the representative of the City of Lille, answered this question in a debate. She had a really good point. She said, "What we have in Lille is not a community-led OFS, but we enable people who otherwise couldn't live in the city center to be part of this community, where we have set up a lot of other participatory instruments. By giving them the opportunity to live there, we also give them the possibility of participating in our city's life." I think that is an interesting point.

Organizing and building where people are poorer and land is cheaper

DAVE SMITH: Now I want to focus on Brussels and, specifically, on Molenbeek. It's a fascinating part of a fascinating city. In the right-wing press in Britain, it gets talked about in unpleasant and, I'd imagine, unfair terms quite a lot. Last year, during the panel discussion on "Building the Beloved Community," you said, "Our main objective, when we started organizing for a community land trust, was to reach those who are in most need."

GEERT DE PAUW: In migrant communities like Molenbeek there's a lot of poverty. But on top of that, there's also a lot of discrimination in housing. It's no wonder that most of the people who are interested in our work and want to get involved, belong to these migrant communities.

DAVE SMITH: I don't know if the politics in Belgium are the same as ours, but it's sometimes very difficult in the UK to do something that appeals to those who are most in need—who, in all likelihood, are frequently migrants—without being seen to be "taking something away" from people in need who are not migrants. Do you have that problem?

GEERT DE PAUW: I remember that you asked me the same question during the panel you moderated on "CLTs and Community Organizing" [laughing]. I didn't really get your question, but now I understand what you mean.

It's important to understand that Brussels is one of the most diverse cities in the world, the second most diverse city in the world after Dubai. There are lots of people living here who weren't born in Belgium. There are also a lot of different nationalities living in Brussels. Even before the migrants, Brussels was already a city where you had different communities living together—French speaking, Flemish speaking.

So I think Brussels has a very open mentality. That doesn't mean there is no discrimination and no racism. But we never had a big nationalist party or racist party that managed to get a minimum of votes. So that shows a lot how Brussels works.

I must say that, in Brussels, it's just accepted that we work with low-income families and migrants. What some people do question, however, is whether low-income families should become homeowners.

DAVE SMITH: That they should remain renters?

GEERT DE PAUW: Yeah. Some people say they should remain tenants, that helping the poor to become homeowners is irresponsible. But the argument that we shouldn't work with them because of not being not born in Brussels, I have never heard that.

DAVE SMITH: You mentioned discrimination. What does that look like?

GEERT DE PAUW: Before I worked in the community land trust, we once did a test where we were calling landlords who had homes for rent. First, someone with an African-sounding name and accent called to ask if the apartment was available for rent. Very often they got the answer that it was already rented out. Then, a few minutes later, I called with the same question. I got the answer that "Yeah, when can you come?" In more than 60% of our calls, the reaction was different when it was someone with a Belgian name and accent who called. It was a very confronting experience.

This is typical and, indeed, can seem contradictory with what I said before. I mean, [laughing], it is not paradise here where everyone loves each other and where there's no racism at all. Not at all. And racism is not necessarily between people born here and people born outside of Belgium. It could also be between other nationalities.

DAVE SMITH: CLT Brussels now works across the whole region. It doesn't just work in one neighborhood. So how does that work? How do you choose where you are going to do your next housing project?

GEERT DE PAUW: Oh well, to be honest it is mainly a question of opportunities. Until now, we have mainly been active in the poorest communities where the land is a bit cheaper than in the richer municipalities in the south. If we would add some kind of strategic elements, we wouldn't get very far. But today we are discussing with a council in a richer municipality, where they are interested in working with us. We would be happy to do that, because it is becoming really difficult to find land.

Dealing with conflict

DAVE SMITH: Do you ever have any conflicts within the CLT? Are there ever any residents or other groups who don't see eye to eye on things? If so, how do they resolve these conflicts—or do you work chiefly by consensus?

GEERT DE PAUW: Hmm, within the central board of the community land trust, up to now, we always manage to decide by consensus.

I don't recall that we ever once ever had to vote for something. So that's something.

DAVE SMITH: We have at least five votes at every meeting at London CLT.

GEERT DE PAUW: Oh, really?

DAVE SMITH: Yeah [laughing]. I'll give you an example. In London, we can't always afford to build all of the houses that are potentially an opportunity for us. We have, like, one group who really wants to build something here. And another group who really wants to build something somewhere else. They are campaigning locally in different parts of the city. It's sometimes quite difficult to make sure that we fairly and democratically resolve where we will allocate our resources. Do you struggle with that kind of problem?

GEERT DE PAUW: I think, as far as I understand the London CLT, you are much more community-led than we are. I mean, for us, these kinds of decisions are made by the board.

But there is a lot of preliminary work that is done by the team and/or by committees. The board doesn't always follow what the team comes up with. But there are not conflicting groups. I don't think you can say that there is a group of residents within the board, then the others, and then those representing the governmental authorities and they disagree. That's not the case.

On the other hand, what's more challenging is at the level of the housing projects. In the preparation, our team plays an important role. In general, it's quite consensual. But once people move into their homes, then it can become more challenging. I must say, however, that I'm really impressed by how residents manage to collectively tackle issues like a small vandalism, or youngsters making noise, et cetera. That can create a lot of tension.

I was recently asked to participate in a residents' meeting a few months ago after there was a lot of fuss, a lot of not-so-nice exchanges on the WhatsApp group of this residential building [laughing]. They invited me as some kind of facilitator. I was really worried to go there.

But it turned out that I was there just as a spectator. They managed to collectively find solutions to these issues. I was really proud of how this worked out. That doesn't mean that we won't have difficulties in the future, but I think it shows that all the time we invest in trainings on nonviolent communication, for instance, and stuff like that really works.

Strategies of organizing and engagement

DAVE SMITH: Hmm. That leads us nicely into a discussion about all the different aspects of that. It strikes me that CLTs are difficult organizations to run. It's hard enough to build affordable housing and to make it stack up financially. And it's hard to run community-led housing and to make sure everybody is involved. Trying to do both in tandem is very challenging.

So I suppose my questions in this area are about how to run a CLT. What are the main obstacles to getting residents involved in CLT Brussels in the planning and management of their own homes? What kind of organizing strategies have proven to be effective in overcoming those obstacles and getting residents involved?

GEERT DE PAUW: My colleagues, over the last couple of years, have really invested a lot of time in looking for the most effective approaches to that—and also trying to standardize the way we work with residents, what kind of trainings we provide, how do we organize meetings, et cetera.

When we started, it was really all about the co-construction of every part of what we did. Now we try to integrate some more systematical approaches, which are being shown to work, I think, but without too much standardizing, of course. You need to be able to adapt to the local situation, the partners you work with, the size of the building, the people in the group, et cetera. But that's something that has really changed in recent years.

DAVE SMITH: I was looking back at what you said in last year's webinar: "People who are applicant homeowners are scattered all over the Brussels region. They belong to different ethnic and cultural communities. So we wanted to create more connections between all these people, amongst all these members. The idea was to be a strong region-wide community, a real movement." As you've gone from working in one small area to working across all of Brussels, how has that changed your community organizing approach?

GEERT DE PAUW: It was more the opposite. When we started, we had some 100 applicants for homeownership, people living somewhere in Brussels. All of them were members. For us, it was very important that applicant homeowners became members, because we think that the voice of those who are in need of housing is very important to be heard in our decision making. But although they were members, most of them were not really involved in our community land trust.

That's why we tried to create a community out of them, trying to connect people and to organize some community activities with them. We wanted to get more people involved in the life of the community land trust and give them a sense of belonging to some wider community. During two years, we invested in strengthening this community of applicant homeowners, using the Asset-Based Community Development method.

There were some positive results out of it. But we didn't really manage to create a movement where everyone who wanted a home and became a member of the CLT would feel part of this movement. We didn't manage to get there at all.

Now, as more and more housing projects are getting developed, we are investing more time and energy in building local communities within the housing projects—and possibly with the communities living around them—rather than trying to invest in a regional movement with all the people.

DAVE SMITH: I suppose that your job as an organizer changes as well. When the CLT is focused on campaigning, it's very much about organizing with people. Then, when you are a house builder, like you are now, you and the community land trust have to sit in middle among the people who are campaigners, the people who want to be residents, the architects, the city government, and the people who give you loans, all these kinds of different things.

GEERT DE PAUW: Yeah, yeah.

DAVE SMITH: I'm interested in your view on that, on how your role as an organizer has changed. Do you still use some of the same organizing tactics?

GEERT DE PAUW: Well, first of all, personally, I'm not as much of an organizer anymore. As CLTB has grown, I took on other roles within the organization. Nevertheless, it's true that our organizing has changed over the years. I already explained it, I think. In the beginning, you could really call it community organizing, where we had the common goal of convincing the authorities to enable creation of a CLT. You could easily call that community organizing. Once the organization was more-or-less settled, it became more about building a community or communities within our housing projects.

I think we have really been quite successful in building communities within those projects, but it will continue to be one of the important challenges for us in the coming years. One of our objectives would also be to connect the different housing projects more to each other.

Our position towards institutions has also changed over the years. If you want to do affordable housing, you need public money. And if you ask for public money, it changes your relationship to the authorities.

But there's also the issue of changing governments and having to build trust each time, having to convince a new government of us being a good solution. There was an interesting episode in our history a few years ago, after we were established. In the beginning, it had it been quite a struggle to convince all the political parties that it would be important to add a community land trust to the housing landscape in Brussels. We more-or-less managed to do that. Then we got another government and the housing minister, let's just say, lost her trust in us. It's a long story, but we really had to go back to organizing strategies again.

At that moment, it was very important to have this broad network of activists, of civil society actors, et cetera. We could go to them and have them discuss CLTB with different people involved in the government. And very slowly we changed the situation.

So it depends on what we are trying to do at the time. On the one hand, it's important to be a trustworthy partner and deliver good housing projects to show that what we do is valuable—and, yeah, be nice [laughing]. On the other hand, you cannot be forgetting that one day the political climate could change. It's important to keep an organization that is resilient and that has a base that can be used whenever it's necessary.

DAVE SMITH: Absolutely. I think you're right to stress that it's not necessarily a contradiction. It's not that you are just doing community organizing, or that you are just being a partner with government. It's a tension that all CLTs exist with the whole time.

Celebrating success

DAVE SMITH: One of the other parts of running a CLT, for me, is the importance of celebration and having a kind of joyousness within it as well. I know that you've done a lot of that kind of community building in Brussels, not just through a sense of struggle, but through a sense of celebration as well.

Whilst I think these things can become too self-congratulatory, too worthy, this work should be a source of joy as well. It's one of the things I've always admired about your work. Is that sense of celebration just a result of the personalities of the people involved with CLTB, or is it a conscious organizing tactic?

GEERT DE PAUW: It's a bit of all that [laughing]. We have always tried to make our general assemblies a moment of celebration. You can combine the strategic thinking and then the party [laughing]. Always every year, we try to get as many people as possible to come to our general assembly. And then we try to make connections between people during a moment of celebration.

So yeah, I think it's essential. For us who are working on this, it's also great to have moments where we can celebrate. We are already starting to prepare for this year's World CLT Day on the 29th of October, for instance, when we want to organize a big party to celebrate our 10th anniversary and the fact that we won the World Habitat Award. We are all very much looking forward to that. And, indeed, we believe these kinds of moments are essential in keeping the movement alive.

DAVE SMITH: Yes, absolutely. The recognition that you got through the World Habitat Award is wonderful and well-deserved. I've known your work for a long time, and I've known others who've worked with you in the organization, but nobody ever said, "We've got a five-year plan to win awards for Brussels Community Land Trust." I know that wasn't your intention, so it's nice when people are recognized.

One last question. You didn't come into this career—or even get into housing—thinking, "Well, it definitely has to be a CLT that I want to do." And knowing you, as I do, you could have made a lot more money working elsewhere and doing other things. Why are you still doing this work? What is it that keeps you going?

GEERT DE PAUW: Hmmm. Well, I think what keeps us going—for all the team and also for the most involved people—is to see what we were dreaming of is really happening today. We are all very proud to see that we have been able to deliver qualitative, affordable housing, but also to see what happens in building communities within that housing. That's something very important, especially with people who are often considered a problem more than a solution. I don't know many other organizations where we would be able to have this kind of impact.

It's also good to see how people have grown within our organization. When we first met them, there were people who hardly dared to say a word. They now take their place on our board. That is something that's really motivating. You start to imagine: If we were able to grow bigger [laughing], what kind of impact could this have on the city?

DAVE SMITH: What's quite telling is that, for a CLT, unlike other housebuilders, it ultimately always comes back to people, doesn't it, rather than buildings? When you're building housing, there's a point at which you stop, but there's no point at which you stop when you're building communities.

6.

A Conversation with Mariolga Juliá Pacheco & Alejandro Cotté Morales, Caño Martín Peña Community Land Trust

Hosted by Line Algoed, February 28, 2022
Translated from Spanish by Zinnia Cintron
Endnotes by Maria E. Hernandez-Torrales

LINE ALGOED: Last year, Mariolga Juliá Pacheco participated in a webinar called "Building the Beloved Community." Alejandro Cotté Morales was a panelist for the webinar devoted to "CLTs and Community Organizing." Today, we are talking with them about community work at the core of the Caño Martín Peña Community Land Trust in San Juan, Puerto Rico and the importance of community organizing in the land trust movement as a whole.[1]

In the Caño Martín Peña, community work is a precondition; there would not be a community land trust without it. So my first question is: In terms of community work, what differences have you noticed between the Caño Martin Peña Community Land Trust and other land trusts in Europe and the United States?

MARIOLGA JULIÁ PACHECO: Compared to other land trusts, I think the main difference is the extent of our community's involvement in decision-making processes. Although community engagement in the governance structure is part of every land trust—at least in the ones we know of—in our case, that involvement is present in all phases. It is not only within the board of directors, but also in phases that may seem very simple. For example, we engage the nearest neighbors in deciding what happens with a vacant lot. In practice, that's how we do it. We include the people who are closest to a particular situation and give them the opportunity to have a say, participating in the decision-making and other tasks related to what is going to happen in that space. This goes beyond a board. Even when the board includes members of the land trust and representation from the larger community, there will always be a more local level of what's happening in those spaces.[2]

We try to engage the community in every aspect, from the design, conceptualization, planning, execution, and assessment of what is being done. This is a challenge. It can slow down decision-making in comparison with other land trusts where the decision-making process might be faster because it has been delegated to an established governance structure. We delegate some decisions to these structures too, but other decisions are developed working side-by-side with the people. That can certainly take more time than in other scenarios.

LINE ALGOED: Why is it important for your land trust to include residents in every aspect?

MARIOLGA JULIÁ PACHECO: When we talk to people as subjects instead of objects, we have to include them in what is going to be developed, not only in assessing the results of what was done. We have to include them and engage them in all phases. In our case, we believe this is also a way of ensuring inclusion, equitable development, and our residents' right to the city.

Governing the land trust and guiding development in the special planning district

LINE ALGOED: What portion of the land making up the special planning district surrounding the waterway[3] is in the land trust?

MARIOLGA JULIÁ PACHECO: A little bit over 280 *cuerdas* are part of the land trust. The whole district is 400 *cuerdas* [approximately 388 acres].

LINE ALGOED: So more than half of the district is now being stewarded by the land trust. That's a rather big surface area of the entire district. Let me ask, do the people who live on the land of the land trust and the ones who live around it have the same voice?

MARIOLGA JULIÁ PACHECO: Only people with a surface rights deed for their home or a formal contract with the CLT are recognized as voting members.[4] When the land trust started, it was an abstraction for a long time, even though it had members. Then it began issuing deeds and started to become much more concrete. Five people got their deeds, then there were ten, then fifteen, then twenty, and then over a hundred. Now there are more than two hundred members.

Those who don't live on the land trust's land don't necessarily have a vote in the formal processes of the CLT's assembly. But anyone can have a voice in the open processes for the district. Everyone is invited, as long as you reside in the district and want to participate and be a part of the process. Your voice will be heard and taken into consideration before final decisionmaking.[5]

ALEJANDRO COTTÉ MORALES: The first option is to find out who are the affected parties around those lands. It doesn't matter if you are a member of the land trust or not. Participants include people from the land trust, members of its board, and community leaders. But what's most important are the people who live nearby, the ones who are going to be directly affected. So, to show them respect, that's the initial process. Then we can work in other ways, with assemblies and other activities if necessary.

MARIOLGA JULIÁ PACHECO: A concrete example, right now, is the Infrastructure Master Plan.[6] There are projects in two particular communities, which will definitely affect some neighborhoods in the district. They won't affect the entire district. And when we held the first round of meetings, the requests from community boards at both G-8 and the land trust,[7] without having talked to each other, without the leaders being in the know, what came out in unison from both boards was: "When the time comes to discuss that issue, we'll do it at that neighborhood's meeting." It was leaders of these community boards who said: "Those of us who live in other streets cannot decide that." So, in that sense, I believe that there is a culture that has been created to include the affected parties in decision-making processes.

ALEJANDRO COTTÉ MORALES: That's very important, because one of the principles has always been that the community is sovereign. The community decides. When we talk about the community, we mean it in a wide sense, the community as a whole. Doing the opposite of that is precisely what most people who own something normally do. There's a traditional hierarchy, where people don't have a say because the land is not theirs.

Here everything is done by consensus. The community is sovereign. The community decides absolutely everything. Yes, there is a land trust and there are people within it. But the land trust responds to the wider community, not only to those members who live on its land. This was created for everyone. The land belongs to everyone. It belongs to all the communities from El Caño.

LINE ALGOED: When do you decide that you've done enough to hear the voices of the community? For example, what if there is a new lot that will be developed? And 20 people come to a meeting, and then another 20 answer a questionnaire. When does the community decide, "Now we know that we can go ahead with that plan?"

MARIOLGA JULIÁ PACHECO: Well, this is going to depend on what they are deciding and the kind of project. For example, the other day we walked around and you took a picture of a sign that said, "Let's all take care of what is ours by taking care of what is yours." It was in front of the urban community garden at Las Monjas. That empty lot was a problem for a very long time. It was a garbage dump for many years. There were many meetings, efforts to save the space, until the very process led to the conclusion: "Look, let's put up a fence. Let's build a fence to avoid more littering."

So it will depend on what is being discussed, its complexity and long-term effect. For example, deciding if a 100-meter lot will become parking a space for two neighboring houses is not the same as talking about building two or three houses on a 400-meter lot. But both are very important.

It's one of our roles to stay out of the back and forth regarding decisions and participation. Many times, we have to be the bad cop and say: "Ok, that is enough, let's affirm the decision and let's move forward. We are not going to get anywhere otherwise." There are people with the best of intentions, who have this puritanical view of participation, so they want to discuss everything all over again. When people are already in the solution phase, they are still in the other stage. In those cases, it's our role to help move the conversation, to go over the agreements and, with the community, to set a path for action or implementation.

ALEJANDRO COTTÉ MORALES: The participatory process is always designed with the community leadership. The leadership is chosen by the community, a leader who represents them in the design process. Wherever we go, if it's in Barrio Obrero Marina,[8] for example, the first thing we ask is, "Who is the community leader here? Look, there is this project, this opportunity. How can we do this?" The same applies if we are in Las Monjas. The leader is approached and then we take it to the community.

The framework of what participation should be is to go first to the street. These residents should decide because they are the ones who will be affected. The rest are informed and asked for general feedback, whether by using a questionnaire or by posting announcements in the community. There are different types of participation. Those who are more affected by a project are encouraged to participate directly.

An example is the hostel.[9] A hostel will be developed, and everyone who lives on that street was consulted first.

LINE ALGOED: Regarding the hostel, was that consultation with the neighbors really done door-to-door? Has everyone on this street been able to participate one way or the other?

MARIOLGA JULIÁ PACHECO: Yes, in that street and in the two adjacent ones.

LINE ALGOED: And you are not finished until everyone has been heard?

ALEJANDRO COTTÉ MORALES: Everyone is informed about what is coming, how it will be done, and how it benefits the community. And they are informed about how they can engage.

MARIOLGA JULIÁ PACHECO: There might be concerns you want to anticipate. What could be the concerns so you can find solutions? Because those will be the oppositions we will encounter. Perhaps they are not opposed to the idea, but they have concerns. How do we address those concerns?

ALEJANDRO COTTÉ MORALES: If we were to go the traditional route, we would not have to go through this process. As I said before, in other places if you're an owner of a building, nobody else should be concerned with what you do with that property. But what do we do here? We respect the people who live nearby and we want to integrate them. This is a collective effort.

Benefits of resident engagement

LINE ALGOED: What benefits does the land trust get by engaging residents? What are the benefits for the organization?

MARIOLGA JULIÁ PACHECO: There are several. First of all, there's the benefit of knowing that we are not making whimsical decisions or decisions based merely on the perceptions of the staff. On the contrary, we make decisions and take steps at the institutional level according to the people's concept and perception of what they want for their community, weighing the advantages and disadvantages of what this entails.

These are not perfect processes; there are many obstacles and challenges in our way. But our intention is to move forward with the people's concepts and hopes for their community. We believe that engaging the community in the planning and execution stages of projects is one of our strengths. In our particular case, it means validation for many generations of Puerto Rican families, and those from other countries, who have lived here and formed these communities. We are acknowledging that they occupy this land and have a right to these spaces, to the city, to health, etc. And the best way to put this into practice is to take their input into consideration in everything that we do. We sometimes get it right. But when we don't, we learn from it and move on.

LINE ALGOED: What are the benefits for the residents living within the land trust district, but who are *not* living on the CLT's lands?

MARIOLGA JULIÁ PACHECO: One of the main benefits for these residents who live within the Special Planning District, but not on the land stewarded by the land trust, is that the land trust works for the general wellbeing of a street, an area, or a vacant lot with potential for development. We're not discriminating based on who is or isn't part of the land trust. On the contrary, we're working precisely in the pursuit of general wellbeing, which is the logic in those participatory processes regardless of the situation or the project we're addressing. So, in that sense, we're definitely contemplating the general wellbeing of a street in a certain project or situation.

That's one aspect. Also, if the land trust has to confront speculation and gentrification as a result of the dredging of the Caño Martín Peña, there will be campaigns and messages in unison in order to protect the community as a whole, not a certain person or family over others. More than half of the land that comprises the Special Planning District is within the land trust and protected by it. If anyone would have the intention to speculate within the District, they would see that there are plans for the District; there is a comprehensive design; there is an entity beyond the residents whose mission is to protect this residential space and to keep the commercial space as a place for small businesses and entrepreneurs and to foster the idea that the space will always belong to the people.

So, in terms of protecting the spaces, it will be more difficult for people with other interests to buy several adjoining properties, for example, hoping to build a new project because there are lands stewarded by the land trust in the entire District. Or, if big developers or speculators wanted to buy a street to demolish the houses and to build a new residential project, they would encounter lands being stewarded by the trust that are right in the middle of it. They would not be able to buy it or they would have to ask for approval from Proyecto ENLACE. And Proyecto ENLACE follows the area's Comprehensive Development Plan and would not grant such an endorsement, since it would go against the community's longterm aspirations for the space.

LINE ALGOED: Mariolga has talked about the benefits for people who live in the district but who are *not* on protected land. Alejandro, now the question for you is: What are the benefits of community work for the people who *are* living on the land stewarded by the land trust? You were part of the second webinar, when the moderator, Dave Smith, posed a rather provocative question. He asked, "What difference does it make, really, for homeowners in a land trust to have an organized community around them? Why do they care for the opportunity to engage in the governance of the land trust? Community participation doesn't make their homes more comfortable or less expensive. Why is it crucial for them to continue to be involved in the land trust's work?"

ALEJANDRO COTTÉ MORALES: An organized community adds value for the entire area. The community becomes a safer place in many aspects, not only in the traditional sense of public safety, but security in where I live. People can engage, as a community, feeling that there's cultural and economic activity. Participating in community organization and development provides a series of things—tools, activities, projects—which are not available in other places.

For people who live on the land, besides having their house as an asset, a benefit of living in an organized community is that they can access resources with less difficulty. They have a place where they can go, where there are people who are organized. I have seen it here. When someone has a particular need, even if it's not within the organization's scope of work, the staff will try to make life easier for that person.

Residents have a more human connection to an institution that is formed by people from their own community and through collaborators who work with the social aspect of human behavior. For Proyecto ENLACE and the land trust, community social work is very important. Other projects are more focused on planning, legal matters, and other things. Here there's a big social work component. Organizational work is definitely very important; it benefits residents in all those aspects: economic, social, cultural, safety concerns.

Even in terms of new housing development, that development responds to the reality of the communities. Community organization is considered also in relocation processes that come up.[10] The leadership responds to the people, and people are sovereign in that sense. It's beneficial to have an organized community. You can see the difference in places where they haven't achieved even 20% of what we have here. Why not? Because they're not organized.

MARIOLGA JULIÁ PACHECO: I also think that, in the case of the people who live on the CLT's land, they know they have our backing. Regardless of any circumstances they might encounter, there are legal resources in place; there are guaranteed rights that are acknowledged by entities designated by the State. (In Puerto Rico, that entity is the Property Registry.) This reassures people because it guarantees that future generations will be able to enjoy their legacy.

ALEJANDRO COTTÉ MORALES: It's about perpetuity. Community participation happens in perpetuity. Community organization is in perpetuity. That is life; it's how it goes; it evolves and is constantly changing. Children have been born and raised here. People have died. So, if you do not keep citizen participation active, who is the project going to respond to? Everything will change.

People will come to live here who have other ideas. They might be good ideas. If it becomes necessary to amend the foundation on which the project was built because there are new people, it'll be done through citizen participation. It won't be done through a traditional hierarchy where Juan or María had an idea and did it this way or that way by finding political support.

When there's an organized force, it must always be active. It must renovate itself constantly, responding to people's reality. And its leadership also needs to be supported. Residents should also be able to question the actions of community leaders, because our leadership could also be swayed by certain political, religious or economic pressures. That's always a danger.

Imagine what would happen if we don't keep citizen participation active. You look at many projects and it isn't active. Twenty years later, there's nothing there; it doesn't exist. It all fell apart because they let the project lose its essence, the reason why it was created in the first place.

And it will come back to bite you, because not keeping participation active devalues the community, it devalues the housing, it devalues culture. You lost it because you made a mistake. There was malpractice at the community planning and community organizing level.

There's also the political context. In Puerto Rico, we live in a colony, within a capitalist system that is constantly prowling, literally, and affecting the more vulnerable people, the communities living in poverty. If you don't have an organized community, this will obviously affect the quality of your work with the communities, because you can't really fight in an organized manner against that oppressive political context.

MARIOLGA JULIÁ PACHECO: Quality of life is not built solely within the four walls of your house. When we talk about improving quality of life, there is an aspect of it that has to do with everything that surrounds us, not only your home's condition or appearance. There are other things that give you a better quality of life, like interpersonal relationships that are built within these spaces surrounding your home that will lead you to say: "No, I'm not leaving my community." All cases are different, but those are the kind of things that together make up your life in community.

Dealing with diversity

LINE ALGOED: Much of the literature about CLTs seems to assume that the community served by a CLT is a homogeneous entity, as if everyone had the same interests and preferences. That does not reflect the reality here in the Caño Martín Peña. How do you manage this diversity within the community?

MARIOLGA JULIÁ PACHECO: We recently had a community meeting where we talked about the first baseball park we're going to build, which will incorporate elements of green infrastructure. While we were discussing this, someone said: "But there are a lot less children here now. Do we really still need a baseball park? There are almost no children left. Who are we building that park for?" We kind of bounced the question back to the person. We said: "Don't adults need recreational spaces as well? And what about the kids who do live here? Even if they're not many, don't they deserve to have a recreational space to spend time with each other, to have fun, to play sports spontaneously?" The person changed their body language and replied: "Well, I hadn't thought about it that way. I only saw the park as a place for kids to play baseball in organized teams."

That's one example. Communities are not homogeneous; they are quite heterogeneous. There are many differences. The fact that the communities have a collective goal doesn't imply that they necessarily agree on everything. In our case, we are eight communities and we are all different. Even the way to summon and to mobilize each community is different. There are some repeated common elements that are successful in mobilization processes, but they're not the same ones in every community.

To think about the community as a single, homogenous entity is a mistake. That is restricting the subjectivity of the very people who make up the community. That is suggesting that everyone thinks the same, which is not real in any place or in any society.

ALEJANDRO COTTÉ MORALES: There's a big floating population of Dominican folks who come to Puerto Rico.[11] And this area is one of many spaces where they come because they have family here, a support system, there are [Dominican] stores nearby. They benefit the community's economy and facilitate the arrival of children and young people. The Puerto Rican population is procreating less. On the other hand, as far as I can see, the Dominican population maybe has more children; we'll see what the census says. But in the case of El Caño, there are many Dominican children.

Some people take root in El Caño, but others use it as a transition. In this area, for instance, or in Barrio Obrero, their kids and grandkids identify themselves as Puerto Rican. Their mom and dad are Dominican, and their grandparents are mostly in the Dominican Republic, but they were born here. They have that Puerto Rican and Dominican mixed culture. While such diversity might be conflicting at times, we have done many activities in El Caño, from literacy programs to sports projects to prevent violence and to promote the integration of race and culture.

We work on different issues in collaborations with the Dominican consulate and with many people related to the settlement, making sure the institutions are designed to respond to them so they can enjoy proper rights and services.

But there's also diversity. We have a very old population, the people who, like Mariolga said, still idealize the origins of the community land trust and its struggles. And then there's the younger population, which is smaller and living through a technological revolution in many aspects. We have been able to retain a lot of them thanks to the community work with young people. You see them evolving in community meetings, in different projects. You see how they get involved.

We've always embraced that diversity and made it part of our work, because it's necessary and it obviously helps us in carrying out new visions. It's very enriching to bring new visions to the project. In that sense, yes, we have done a lot of work and we're still working. We've gone from people having a sense of ownership and belonging to the space to now seeing ourselves as part of the city; not like a small island in a corner, but as part of San Juan.

MARIOLGA JULIÁ PACHECO: That heterogeneity is also reflected in the land trust's leadership. We are often asked, for instance, with regard to our Dominican population: "How are they included?" Well, it's an open process. When you look at the community leadership profile in the last assembly, between 33% and 35% of the community leadership are Dominicans or of Dominican descent in 2022. So you explain to people: If roughly between 20% and 30% of the District's population is Dominican, and 33% to 35% of its leadership is of Dominican descent, then they are represented. There is representation according to demographic diversity.

And the same applies in terms of age groups. We need to keep working on how to integrate different generations, but you can see it reflected in community meetings.

That's where we come in as community social workers. We strive to keep those interests, that balance of interests and activities, those integration processes, training new leaders to complement those who have been here for twenty years. Because, obviously, a leader who's been part of the organization for twenty years and who's gone through many processes of exchange with other communities will have developed a better understanding of the project and will have learned public speaking skills, for example.

More than 60% of our CLT members are over sixty years old. If we see them, as it often happens in society, as older people who are retired and don't have much to contribute, then we're missing an organizational force that's willing and able, that's hungry to help the community in any way they can. Each one from where they are, their reality.

LINE ALGOED: Has the land trust prioritized any particular group within the community on the grounds of income, for example?

MARIOLGA JULIÁ PACHECO: No. Homeowners are homeowners. For instance, right now we're looking at the rules on improvements in the household economy to make sure they are not penalized. Our intention is to make sure that future generations will get to stay here.

We have young people who have gone through different community processes and are now professionals, who are the first generation. They work here or in other spaces.[12] And if the land trust were going to develop housing with exclusions on account of income on 100% of the units we build, we would be excluding people who grew up here, who are now professionals, people who we need to keep contributing to the community and the country.

We're really aware of this, of how to keep the balance, considering the fact that the district will be populated eventually by a new group of people. Not today, not tomorrow, but in the long term the district will see demographical changes with new people moving to the area. So who do we want to attract? These conversations are just beginning, they are still in their infancy. But the issue is present.

ALEJANDRO COTTÉ MORALES: We have a few people who had two or three houses on the land when it was acquired by the land trust. These are people who had the opportunity to thrive and to earn some extra money. They could have left. But they stayed in the community. They stayed and contributed to the community, unlike other places where you bring people from the outside and they end up displacing the locals. These people didn't do that. They ended up offering accessible housing, either selling it to people from the community at an affordable price or renting it for a modest fee.

So there are people who were born and raised here. Other people come to live here. Some of them have children and decide to stay here. As long as there's the possibility to keep respect towards the people who lived here, the original ones, obviously the people who come will strengthen us. But if you don't have a basic structure of respect, then the project loses its purpose.

Managing divisions and conflicts

LINE ALGOED: How do you handle division within the community? If there were, for example, some residents who wanted the land trust to do one thing and other residents who wanted something different?

MARIOLGA JULIÁ PACHECO: Where possible, we try to reach an agreement. We do so through different participatory techniques and methodologies. You can use different techniques according to the type of workshop, the issue to be addressed, and the population. Mediation, consensus, confrontation. It will depend on the issue. There's not a single answer. It will greatly depend on the issue.

If you can reach an agreement, great. If not, then you need to have a voting process, right? And if that happens, then you need to protect people who have different opinions. You could have two very strong leaders in a discussion, for example, who can intimidate people who would not dare to vote against them. When there is a conflict, therefore, it's sometimes necessary to vote in secret. We also need to always take into account the level of literacy. In those spaces, we encounter all levels of literacy, and we have to guarantee an inclusive process in which anyone and everyone can integrate and be a part of decision-making processes.

Our goal is to mediate in order to get the purest decision in terms of the participatory process. Without resorting to participatory puritanism or creating a participatory bubble, we encourage people to express what they really feel and think.

ALEJANDRO COTTÉ MORALES: You have to look at each case on its own. If it doesn't affect the community as a whole, where it's an issue between two people that has nothing to do with community development, we try to reach an agreement between them (with courts being the last resort).

But when it's about a common space or common land, and everyone is affected, we hold meetings. Along with the community's leadership, community social workers facilitate a process of discussion to talk about the best use for that space and what is causing the conflict.

We live in a society where everyone is getting more aggressive. Years ago in Puerto Rico, you could work things out. People had a way of sitting down and putting differences aside. There was more space for discussion. Nowadays, everyone is always in a rush. The rush is so intense that people are pretty much drained and the first thing that comes out of their mouth is an insult.

In our community processes we say, "Forget about that, we'll figure something out." In that sense, I think the community has always been a mediator in many aspects. The final decision is made collectively. When someone comes with economic self-interests, for example, the community notices and takes a stand by telling them: "Hold on. This is either for everyone or for no one."

MARIOLGA JULIÁ PACHECO: Conflicts are part of the job. I believe that confronting them is a good thing because they show that you are moving forward. If you are stagnant, you will not be confronted by conflicts because you've already solved them. Whenever there is no conflict should be times to wonder: "Wait a minute, why aren't there problems here? Why are there no obstacles here? What are we not doing?" Changes bring about tension, and tension causes conflicts. It's part of what one encounters in collective and community processes.

LINE ALGOED: Do you think there are people who feel excluded or threatened by the processes of the land trust? For example, people not in the land trust who have individual title to real estate in the district, who might think that the land trust is going to take over all the land.

ALEJANDRO COTTÉ MORALES: There are always people like that. Some people act a certain way because of fear, natural fear, because it was too much too soon, too many facilitators from inside and outside. At first, it could have been assumed that we were speculators, that we worked for the bank, or we were people who had other political and economic interests.

But as you start working on it, you go inside the conflict. Dialogues arise, and people from the community begin to feel less anxious. People contribute, then they can see results brought on by their decisions. Some begin to join because they see it's genuine, that the work is being done in service to the community.

Others remained with their politicians of the day, mainly from rightwing parties, and kept making trouble. We had to fight that a lot here. We experienced that with a former mayor, Jorge Santini.[13] Many people were afraid, which is normal because they disappeared from the community. These agitators sowed discord and generated concerns for many older people.

When you work with people on an individual or collective level, they appreciate it. "Look, you helped me with this. Look, the community leader is involved with that. I believe in that leader." And those anxieties and fears calm down, but they will always exist. That is normal because what you are doing affects their status quo.

MARIOLGA JULIÁ PACHECO: If we said the contrary, that these fears and antagonisms will not occur, we would just be idealizing the process. That is not reality. There will always be differences of opinions. There will always be people who see things differently. And there will always be people opposed for any number of reasons: partisan political reasons; religious reasons; life vision; cosmovision; nostalgia; resistance to change.

The role of outside professionals in supporting community leadership

LINE ALGOED: Could you talk about the role you play, as community workers, and the roles played by other professionals who live outside of the Caño in supporting the projects of ENLACE and the land trust?

ALEJANDRO COTTÉ MORALES: Professionals from all disciplines need to understand that they will be facilitators. We must be careful. Whenever the community's leadership is fearful because they think they don't know something, they pass the question to a professional. And the professional, instead of bouncing it back to the community, tends to answer with recommendations all around. That can happen.

Here at El Caño, we're very careful about that. No matter which field they come from, professionals should always respond to the community instead of imposing their own judgment. They should only be facilitators. It's a delicate issue. We need to ask the community. If the community says no, then no it is. We can do a pros and cons exercise, but the decision is not ours. The community has the final say, even if we do not agree with their decision. So, internally, we must pay attention to this as well.

MARIOLGA JULIÁ PACHECO: We need to keep our expectations in check, in light of what the community wants. Some people classify the staff as centrist, centrist-leftist, or leftist, because it's a group of progressive and liberal people for the most part. But what you and I think is not necessarily what the community thinks. So, how do we respect that boundary between my beliefs, my world view, and what the community sees? As Alejandro was saying, you can evaluate situations, you can list pros and cons. But, at the end of the day, I go home to Trujillo Alto every night.[14] I don't stay here.

ALEJANDRO COTTÉ MORALES: You can't go to a street or knock on people's doors if you are not from here. First of all, they are not going to open the door. And they will not give you any information because they say to themselves, "I don't know who you are." They are also protective of their home. We all are. But when you say, "I am this person's daughter; you are a neighbor; we are leaders from the G-8." They say, "Yes, of course, this benefits the community."

At first, it's always a joint effort with the community leadership. Eventually, though, you can perhaps go as an employee of Proyecto ENLACE or the land trust, even if you don't live here because a member of the community has opened the door for you. Conversely, there are things that the leadership, who are volunteers, aren't obligated to do because it's the job of an employee who gets paid to do it. But everything is done according to the instructions and through a process established with the community's leadership.

MARIOLGA JULIÁ PACHECO: What Alejandro brought up is very important because community leaders are volunteering their time after working their jobs, after their frenzied days, after taking care of a bedridden person. We're here doing a paid job to implement certain tasks, respecting the process, working alongside the community and letting them lead the way. When we do things does not mean that there was no participation. There was participation in the design, execution, and assessment. But we would not expect for people who are volunteering their time to also fill out 400 questionnaires. No, we do it together and we figure out how to balance the load.

The way I see it, part of our role is to figure out how to include people who are very busy, who have many jobs. How do we involve them?

And how do we achieve generational integration, instead of just handing over leadership of the land trust, out with the old and in with the new? As staff, we challenge the leadership to do different things and to think about who we're working for. We sometimes get stuck in nostalgia for what used to be: "No, we can't do that because it was done this way before." Yes, but there's other people now. Other people with a different view of life are living here now. How do we keep that balance between what was, respecting our origins and what gives us strength, while also letting people into leadership who are going to give us a new direction?

ALEJANDRO COTTÉ MORALES: The community's leadership tends to err on the side of being linear: "What does the law say? What does this paper say?" They want to go by the book to follow what's on paper. They go and find a lawyer who steps in to complicate things even more. But this is about human relations, about people. This is the basis of community work. Nothing should be above it, nothing at all.

That's a constant battle in the community organization processes. We have excellent leaders, but they can sometimes be linear. And then they look for lawyers who confuse them and then they say, "It's the word of a lawyer; it's the word of God." No, the decision is yours. The community has the floor. The community is God. The community is sovereign.

MARIOLGA JULIÁ PACHECO: It happens with lawyers, but also with other professionals. For example, if we look at developing new housing, the urban planning group is dying to build three houses on a certain lot. But the leadership says: "No, you are building two." So, every chance they get, the planning group reiterates: "Well, on that lot where we could have built three houses, the community decided to build two."

We have to tell them: "And why did they decide that? So that they can serve as model houses, as guides, so that people can come around, see them, and want to live there." Your urbanist mind says: "Let's build three because we can densify that way." But the leadership sees it differently. What they're considering goes beyond densification. They want their people to choose these houses. They will do this if the houses turn out right, if they look attractive, so that people will say: "Damn, if I get one of those houses from Proyecto ENLACE, built by the land trust, I'll be all right." And that response is more important than constructing a larger number of houses.

Strategies for overcoming obstacles and sustaining resident engagement

LINE ALGOED: What are the main obstacles to engaging residents in the planning and governance of the land trust?

ALEJANDRO COTTÉ MORALES: Time, as you can imagine. People who live in poverty have two or three jobs. They have too much to worry about, rather than to think about going to a meeting, no matter how good or how important it is. They are tired after work. Time, people's availability, the socioeconomic crisis they live every day in this country. In order for them to come, you need to establish different strategies, since meetings are usually held at night or in the late afternoon.

Sometimes partisan politicians create obstacles, either because they have an agenda or because the land trust gets in the way of their interests. There are people in the community who answer to those political leaders and they tend to spread misinformation. That also limits the number of people who participate because sometimes they see these politicians as leaders they must follow. There is a culture of answering to political parties from within the family, from the moment you are born until you die. So that's one of the obstacles.

Another obstacle is trying to do too many activities at the same time and expecting participation in all of them. We need to make the community's leadership understand that there are different types of participation. It is unrealistic to expect 80 out of 100 families to attend any meeting. There is growing insecurity in many aspects of people's lives. "I have two jobs, three jobs, and I'm also supposed to go to a meeting? If it's not relevant, then I'm not going."

LINE ALGOED: What are the most effective strategies to overcome these obstacles, so there's community participation and engagement?

MARIOLGA JULIÁ PACHECO: It will depend on the issue. But people need to feel your honesty as an entity and as individuals who work for that entity. When we make announcements, we disclose the issue we will be discussing. We are strict about this, so people know the reason for the meeting. We must respect the people who came to participate specifically because of the issue at hand. We must be transparent in this journey and process. People must know the purpose of the meeting, their time must be respected, and their opinions must be validated.

We also intervene when someone hijacks the conversation. That role of intervening, so that other people can participate, is very important.

ALEJANDRO COTTÉ MORALES: Recruitment is important. Recruiting both professional staff as well community leadership is key. This is not for everyone. I would dare to use the word *idealization*. Communities can be idealized. "Look, how cute; the community is organized." Well, it's not like that. That did not happen by the grace of the Holy Spirit. It happened because of community organizers. People talk about "organic processes," but there's always someone driving things, facilitating things.

Ander said: "Participation is not spontaneous and natural. You have to create it. You have to pave the way." While I disagree with Ander on some points, I agree with him on this one.[15] You have to pave the way, create spaces, and keep these spaces in constant evolution.

Obstacles are overcome by having key people who can work for and respond to the community. The community makes every decision, but there needs to be professionals in the field of human behavior and community social work to support them.

Another thing, the leadership must recruit new people. It must renew itself constantly so it's not appointed in perpetuity. We have some leaders who have served this community for 20 or 30 years, but that's different because people choose them. Not many people want that job. So the leadership must be renewing itself all the time with the support of professionals who will reinforce them and offer their assistance.

Human resources are key. The community leader is a key human resource. The alliances you will create are key. You address challenges by making alliances. We have alliances with great people in several areas: finances, culture, politics, the private sector, and government. Without alliances nothing would have been accomplished.

We must also be respecting and understanding the different types of participation. We have been led to believe that participation necessarily implies people attending meetings or assemblies. Since we started here, however, we have seen different types of participation and they are all equally valuable. The person who took their kids to a sports event hosted by the CLT, for example, that is participation. They took a couple of hours from their time, putting their personal budget at risk. The kids' event led to a process of discussion because it's not about sports just for the sake of sports, it's about incorporating different strategies. That is a win right there.

We can't overlook the value of someone who talked and gave their opinion while staying home, or the people who have cooked for activities. We're always working with the leadership, explaining that they should not feel frustrated if not everyone attended a meeting.

There is no system appealing to individuality, so people go to meetings to spend maybe two hours getting bored.

The important thing is to inform the rest of the community afterwards. Those decisions always go to the grassroots. When they are making fundamental decisions, they always have to go the grassroots. They held a meeting, went door-to-door or prepared a questionnaire. Never has an important issue been decided by the 20, 30 or 50 people who attended a meeting. Never.

LINE ALGOED: How do you retain participation in the long term while avoiding burnout? How do you keep the residents committed for the long run?

MARIOLGA JULIÁ PACHECO: I think that members with title deeds are a bit easier to retain because they already have that security, that piece of paper guaranteeing that their future generations will inherit the land. But it's a bit more difficult with the people who do not have their deeds yet, who are not certain of their ownership, who are not sure that it will not be taken away.

But we are constantly learning from the leadership. How to overcome obstacles, how to work around issues, how they never quit, how they are still here after 20, 25 or 30 years. We can really acknowledge the time they invest, their value, and their contributions. Walking together, side by side, they know they can count on us. We are not here merely for meetings and decision-making. If you are in the hospital, everyone here will be watching out for you. And when you come out: "Do you have something to eat? We have this and that soup, I'll bring you some. Which one do you want?"

It's just about looking after this human being, beyond their role, beyond the decisions they make in certain times and spaces. And acknowledging their value as a person. The sacrifices they make and the time they invest to be here.

LINE ALGOED: For many CLTs, the participation of residents is mainly a matter of giving them a voice in the elections, a place on the CLT's board. Other aspects of community development can take a back seat. We see that in many CLTs. That's not the case in El Caño, however. What other opportunities and spaces have you created at the Caño CLT so that the residents are constantly connected to the land trust?

ALEJANDRO COTTÉ MORALES: The leadership is constantly asked to work, just work. Forget about recreation. That's a luxury for our people. Some people put in 20, 30 or 40 hours of volunteer work weekly. But the leadership needs recreational spaces that let them unwind. So every year they get to stay in a hotel for three days to relax and to have fun, while in trainings. And there are other activities such as Christmas parties or having breakfast together, like we used to do at the beginning and still do. By providing spaces that recognize their work and that allow them to have fun, we keep the group integrated.

MARIOLGA JULIÁ PACHECO: Group cohesion is about having a laugh together, about relaxing. We have privileges that many people do not have, so we sometimes find tickets to the movies for young people to go watch a good movie together as a group. All of these things are very important and are part of the work plan for the G8, the land trust, and Proyecto ENLACE. To have a laugh—or sometimes a cry when someone is going through a difficult situation. All that promotes great solidarity and support among the community's leadership.

Notes

1. *Fideicomiso de la Tierra del Caño Martín Peña* (Caño CLT) comprises seven communities within the Caño Martín Peña Special Planning District. Each community has its own needs, which are addressed in the Comprehensive Development Plan and Land Use Plan for the Caño Martín Peña Special Planning District. This Plan was designed by the community with the help of urban planners, engineers, and architects, among other professionals.

2. The Caño CLT board of trustees has a different composition than the tripartite structure of the "classic" CLT. Residents living on the land trust's land constitute a majority of the board, not just a third.

3. The Caño Martín Peña Special Planning District is located along the Martín Peña waterway ("Caño" in Puerto Rican Spanish).

4. The surface rights deed is the legal document used by the Caño CLT, instead of the land lease agreement used by other CLTs. In Puerto Rico's Property Registry Law, the surface rights deed is the legal instrument that recognizes the member's individual right to the house and right to use the collectively owned land.

5. The CLT General Regulations is the source of the right to be heard of those living within the Caño Martín Peña Special Planning District, regardless of whether they are on the CLT's land.

6. The Master Plan guides the construction of new water, power, and road infrastructure needed to keep the Martín Peña channel clean after it has been dredged. There are cases where projects are specific for one or two communities and not for the whole Special Planning District. The infrastructure works are the responsibility of the government, but the community organization and the Caño CLT make sure those projects are conducted according to the infrastructure master plan.

7. G-8 is the Group of the Eight Communities, which includes the Caño Martín Peña, Inc. G-8 brings together all the grassroots initiatives in the district. This group was established before the CLT. In fact, it was the organizing and planning done by G-8 that led to the creation of the Caño CLT.

8. Barrio Obrero Marina is one of the eight communities along the Martín Peña channel. The other communities are Barrio Obrero San Ciprián, Las Monjas, Buen Vista Santurce, Israel

& Bitumul, Buena Vista Hato Rey, Parada 27, and Península de Cantera.

9. The hostel is a project developed by the G-8. Their goal is to have a place to host those who come to the community to learn about the CLT and about other community projects, while generating funds for the G-8 and creating some jobs.

10. As part of the dredging of the Martín Peña channel, several households living closest to the waterway are being relocated with the help of staff from Proyecto ENLACE. Some may be relocated within the district if they so wish. This process is supported by a committee partly composed of residents who have gone through relocation themselves.

11. These are immigrants from the Dominican Republic.

12. They work at the Proyecto ENLACE Corporation, or the Caño CLT, or the G-8, Inc.

13. Jorge Santini was the Mayor of San Juan, Puerto Rico from 2004 to 2012.

14. Trujillo Alto is a suburb of San Juan.

15. Ezequiel Ander-Egg is a philosopher, teacher, sociologist, and essayist, born in Argentina in 1930. He has authored more than one hundred books on social, economic, and educational topics, including *Historia del Trabajo Social* (History of Social Work).

7.

A Conversation with Ashley Allen, Houston Community Land Trust

Hosted by John Emmeus Davis
March 22, 2022

JOHN EMMEUS DAVIS: I want to begin our conversation today pretty much where we began the webinar last year, when you spoke about your early experiences as a community organizer. You had lived in a couple of homeless shelters as a youth. You later became an organizer for the Coalition for the Homeless in Chicago. During our webinar you said that working with the Coalition for the Homeless was your way of coping with the experience of having been homeless and allowed you to "get involved and to make change." What kind of "change" were you trying to make with the Coalition for the Homeless?

ASHLEY ALLEN: Well, the first thing that was significant for me in becoming a community organizer was to change the stigma and the stereotype of what it means to experience homelessness.

We have this very narrow view as a society of who is homeless or why someone is homeless. I am college educated, you know. I now have a decent job. The assumption would not be that I had spent a good portion of my life couch-surfing and living in shelters and things of that nature.

My mother worked and was really committed to keeping a job, but she just didn't make enough money. Some people think all homeless people have mental health issues or drug addiction, you know, things like that. But that wasn't the case for us. And that wasn't the case for a lot of families that were in the shelters that we were in. It was just changing life circumstances, a drop in income, loss of a job, or working a job that would not meet the needs of supporting a household.

So that was when I got involved, that was something that was very important to me, changing what people thought about homelessness.

JOHN EMMEUS DAVIS: Did it take awhile for you to come to that sense of personal empowerment, so that you could share your story and get past the stigma of homelessness?

ASHLEY ALLEN: I wanted to be able to feel comfortable telling my story. I hid it from my own family. My mom's sisters and my cousins had no idea of the extent to which we were homeless. They had no clue how bad it had gotten because they didn't live in the same city as us. My mother was very private about what was happening and in what people got to know.

I took on that. You don't tell anybody. You don't talk about it. I have friends, 30-year friends, who are just now finding out about my experience. I've known them since middle school and they just found out.

JOHN EMMEUS DAVIS: What sort of organizing did the Coalition do? What was your approach to community organizing in those days?

ASHLEY ALLEN: Well, the first thing I will say is that I really appreciated that they taught us how to be organizers. They didn't just throw us out there and say, "Hey, go make change." They taught us about the history of organizing and what it looked like, particularly in Chicago. We were talking about Saul Alinsky. And we were talking about employees' unions and things like that, how organizing truly got started and what that meant.

People often talk about getting out and making change and a lot of times it's like, "Well, okay, should I just go march? Should I just go protest? Should I go to my legislator? How does that work?" So they taught us about the history of organizing and common strategies of organizing.

The first thing that has been the most beneficial to me in all of my jobs—not just as a community organizer, but also as a nonprofit professional—is building relationships. What does that mean? It means when you're going into a room, even if it's going into a room to cause some tension to build, it means starting off with relational questions. How do we connect? What are our common goals? What are our common interests?

That was one thing that I learned. When you're going into a room, whether it's with an ally or an adversary, to start with those conversational and relational questions so that you find your common ground. Because eventually either you're going to end up diverging on a particular topic or you're going to be coming together on a particular topic, but you always start with that relationship.

JOHN EMMEUS DAVIS: Has that carried over to the present? Alinsky-style organizing is a much more adversarial approach. Your organizing approach at the Houston CLT is different today, yes?

ASHLEY ALLEN: No. Because sometimes you're coming in and you're trying to find that common ground, but you're understanding that there may be a point in which there's no common ground. And then that Alinsky approach of being a little bit more adversarial, being a little bit more militant in your ask, has to happen.

One of the major things that the Coalition for the Homeless did was policy change. It wasn't just let's get more services. We were talking about changing policy. There was the "Fight for 15" to increase the minimum wage so that people could actually have enough money to prevent becoming homeless, to have enough money to live.

One of the things that I worked on specifically, since I was in the education department, was creating temporary living-situations policy for students. At the federal level, there's the McKinney-Vento Act that is supposed to protect students in public schools and their families who are experiencing homelessness, making sure that their educational experience isn't tainted because they are experiencing homelessness. But the City of Chicago had not revised their students-in-temporary-living-situations policy. So there were a lot of students who didn't know they could get bus cards to go to school. They didn't know that their school fees should be waived. They didn't know things like being able to walk in graduation if you didn't have the money or being able to attend prom if you didn't have the money.

Those are some of the things that were supposed to be included in the City's policy. But the policy had not been rewritten in 20 years and nobody was using it. So all these students were like, "Why are we being punished for our address not matching our school? Yeah, well, I'm homeless. Therefore, my address may not match my school because I'm living with my aunt today. I'm living in the shelter tomorrow. I'm living with grandma in three weeks." They shouldn't be punished for that.

I spent a year-and-a-half with a great team going to the City, going to the City's chief of staff. At that time, Rahm Emanuel was the Mayor of Chicago. So we were working with his chief of staff and working with his director of education to get this policy rewritten.

And we got a lot of push-back. You would think it wouldn't be hard to get policies to support students that were experiencing homelessness. But it was 18 months of back and forth, getting them to understand why they were in violation of the federal McKinney-Vento Act by not having a local policy and, also, what was the true impact on someone's education when they have unstable housing.

And so, for me, being able to tell my story about the impact of unstable housing on my own education was very helpful. Bringing in real life sometimes helps people who are just policy wonks to understand the real implication of the lack of a policy. I understand policy because that's my academic training, but I was also able to bring in that real world experience, to kind of bring them together to say, "All right, this is why this is important, because this is what its implication is for a student if you do not include it."

There were definitely some very contentious moments. I showed up, along with a lot of other organizers, at school board meetings and going back and forth. I remember one of the school board members saying, "Oh, well, if there's so many homeless students, why don't you name them?" And I lost it. I was very angry. Basically, my response was, "How dare you make people have to expose something so sensitive to prove something that we know to be true." We know that there are at least 20,000 homeless students in the Chicago Public Schools. Most people don't even report it because they're too ashamed. Or they don't understand that being doubled up is considered homeless. Or they are scared their kids will be taken away if people know about their living situation.

So, again, you have a relational start in hopes that somebody will listen and that this connection will move the conversation forward. But you also have an understanding that those methods used by Saul Alinsky are sometimes necessary because you are going to have to push back.

Community organizing versus resident engagement

JOHN EMMEUS DAVIS: Jump forward now to your time here at the Houston Community Land Trust. How has your approach to organizing changed? Or has it? The relational elements, the policy advocacy, the telling of powerful personal stories to convince public officials—some of those elements have been carried forward in the work you do today. Yes? Is what you are doing different today that different than what you were doing in Chicago?

ASHLEY ALLEN: I don't think it's very different. I came in with the idea that I wouldn't have to do the fighting that I did in Chicago with city government, because the city government was supporting our program.

JOHN EMMEUS DAVIS: When you came to the Houston CLT?

ASHLEY ALLEN: When I came to the Houston CLT. I didn't think I would have to do the same fighting that I did in Chicago. That is one of the reasons why I took this job. I'm like, "Hey, I finally get to be working together to do good. I don't have to be the troublesome person always showing up at school board meetings and, you know, getting a little rowdy."

But because of changing leadership that recently happened within Houston's housing department, some more direct organizing had to be done. Not organizing per se, not having to bring people in as we did in Chicago, but that step right before. We're saying to the City, "This is where the problem is, and we're looking to you to help us. Let's come to an agreement before I have to call in the people and call in the organizers and we have to start taking things to a higher level."

That's kind of where we are right now, I'm going to be honest. That's where I am in the process right now, hoping that I don't have to rely on the relationships that I've built, asking our coalition of people to help in forcing the City's hand.

Those same strategies may not work as well in Houston, but what has worked is building relationships so that I have support. If we need them, I have people who will be rallying and supporting us and who are able to understand the implications of policies that do not benefit us. We're able to communicate that to the City, which is why the City's willing to have those conversations.

JOHN EMMEUS DAVIS: Ashley, I was struck in the earlier webinar by the distinction you drew between community engagement and community organizing—and your assertion that one can complement the other. It seems to me that's what you're talking about here. You've put time into community engagement: building relationships, building that base of trust and support. So now, if you need to reach back and to ask your supporters to act in a more adversarial fashion, pushing the city government a little more, you've got that in reserve. Am I hearing you correctly?

ASHLEY ALLEN: Absolutely. That's exactly how I make that distinction. Engagement is the relationship-building part and organizing is the action.

You develop engagement in a group that supports you and sees your vision and wants to work toward a similar vision. In Houston, I'm able to build those relationships because we're all trying to provide affordable housing. How does the CLT complement what you're already doing? Great. Well then, here's how we can help you. Let's have this conversation.

For instance, one of our housing partners said we really need to figure out how we're going to get permitting fixed here in Houston. And I said, "Absolutely, let's have that conversation." So when I had my next meeting with a City Council member I said, "You know, one of the things that I would really like to get some information on is your permitting process down in the Planning Department. What's going on?" And I was able to get more insight and to ask, "Hey, can we get the City Council on board in creating a more streamlined process for affordable housing builders, particularly nonprofit builders? You are all saying you want to improve the amount of affordable housing, but you're holding up the people who are doing it. That's not really helping your cause of getting more affordable housing."

So I'm advocating for them. Then I turn around and say, "Hey, I'm getting ready to meet with the Mayor. I really need for you to get him to understand why the CLT model needs to continue. We need to remove barriers to applications from people who want to get downpayment assistance for CLT homes." And they said, "If you need a letter of support, we'll do it. Let us know what else we can do."

So, for multiple organizations, I advocate for them; they advocate for me. Then, together, we're making the changes we ultimately need. We can then all get to the same goal, which is more affordable housing on the ground.

Organizational benefits of resident engagement

JOHN EMMEUS DAVIS: You have a base of support that you can call upon to make policy change and to get public money. That is a clear benefit to your organization from cultivating a community base. What are some other benefits of resident engagement? How does that help the Houston CLT?

ASHLEY ALLEN: Well, for one, it helps to maintain that support, because you don't want to be spending money, particularly public dollars, if you don't have the impact that the community has suggested. In the fundraising space, while we appreciate fundraising dollars from foundations and all they do, I've noticed that sometimes they're so comfortable in only funding things they're familiar with or using the same funding strategy.

For instance, with housing the most common thing is, "Oh, let's do financial literacy and homebuyer education." Great. Fantastic. We definitely want educated buyers. We support that. We want financially stable buyers. We support that. But at what point do we move past just saying, "Hey, get your credit in order?" When do we actually get homes on the ground? And when we finally get people in them, how do we actually support people once they're in their homes?

That's what people are asking for. Nobody's coming up to me and saying, "You know, what I really need and what this community really needs is a homeowner education class." They're saying, "I need housing that I can afford on my current job or my fixed income. I need more development in my community to make it safe." That's what they're saying. They're not saying anything about homebuyer education or financial literacy.

By having homeowners and community members on our board, by really focusing on community engagement, you get to hear what people truly need. You're not guessing or using the path of least resistance because getting affordable housing is hard. Homebuyer education is quite easy to do. There are tons of people who do it and do it very well. It's easy to fund, because it's something where you're going to see immediate results, but it's still not addressing the community's needs. We want to make sure, as a CLT, that the community's needs are being heard and that we're actually giving them what they're asking us for, which is more affordable housing for limited-income individuals.

JOHN EMMEUS DAVIS: Community involvement helps you to prioritize your program, your mix of services; it provides a kind of a built-in feedback loop. Right? What I hear you saying is that your residents will tell you when you're hitting the mark and when you're not, and what their highest priorities and needs might be.

ASHLEY ALLEN: Yeah. Right. For instance, one of the reasons why we didn't start off automatically with a stewardship program was because we had only five homeowners. Who's going to determine what the stewardship program looks like? I've developed a lot of programs, but I don't ever want to develop a program just based off my experience. I knew we needed a stewardship program, but I didn't think we could build a quality stewardship program until we had enough homeowners to basically tell us what their needs are.

So I said to my staff, once we have enough homeowners to really to see what issues come up, what workshops they would like, what events they would like, then we can build out a robust stewardship program. And I think that approach has worked because now we're able to really focus on the things they want and need.

JOHN EMMEUS DAVIS: Does community sometimes get in the

way? Do you ever get pushback from other people at the City or at foundations or at the land bank who say, "Look, you would be a much more efficient provider of affordable housing if you didn't include all of these people in your decision-making and on your board. The 'C' in CLT slows everything down." Do you ever hear that?

ASHLEY ALLEN: I don't hear that. Instead, the pushback comes from more established organizations believing they do it better. And the City, of course, is like, we've been doing it this way for decades; what makes you think you can come in and make things more efficient? The push-back was around this community-based organization coming in and trying to tell them how to do downpayment assistance better and how to help people to get into housing. If we look at the track record, I do believe that we have proven to be more efficient, while really giving the community what they ask for and what they need, not just doing what's been done for decades that may not be as effective.

That happens more so with the bigger entities, people who have done affordable housing forever. Some of these developers don't believe in the CLT model because they don't understand why a homeowner wouldn't own the land. They've been doing affordable housing the same way for decades. But their inventory of affordable housing is negative because they've been putting in $30,000 or $40,000 and then the house is back on the traditional market. And then you're giving somebody else another $30 - $40,000 to buy a house and the same thing happens. It doesn't make sense. But, again, you're not thinking about what the community wants, which is a place to be stable, to not get kicked out, to be able to afford it today and tomorrow.

JOHN EMMEUS DAVIS: So the pushback is more around the CLT's form of tenure, about the separation of land and buildings and the commitment to permanent affordability. It's not, "Why are you involving all those people in the governance of your organization?" It's not push-back around community engagement per se.

ASHLEY ALLEN: Yes, but they use community as their reason.

They use community not to say they're getting in the way, but to question whether or not we're truly helping. The community is used to push-back against the CLT. They say, "You're not really helping the community because you're not allowing them to own the land; you are not really helping them build wealth." Or, "You're not educating them enough. They don't know what they're getting into."

You know, people in the community aren't idiots. They might not understand the CLT model perfectly. (I've been doing this for years, and I still don't understand everything about the CLT model.) But they are definitely getting enough of an education and understanding of the CLT for them to make an informed decision about whether this is best for them and their family.

JOHN EMMEUS DAVIS: Community becomes the catch-all excuse for criticizing the CLT. Interesting. Let me ask about community involvement from the point of view of your homeowners. How many homeowners do you have at this point?

ASHLEY ALLEN: Seventy-five. We now have seventy-five homeowners.

JOHN EMMEUS DAVIS: From the point of view of those homeowners, I want to go back to the provocative question that Dave Smith asked during your webinar. What difference does it actually make to CLT homeowners for there to be a community-led organization standing behind the deal. Why should they care about community organizing? After all, they're in a nice home; it's secure; it's warm—or, in your case, it's air-conditioned. Why should they care that there is a community land trust standing behind them?

ASHLEY ALLEN: That is one of the things that we want to work on. We want to get them to understand they are part of something bigger. At the annual holiday party that we have for residents, we always try to make sure that we talk about it being something bigger. And once they see how many homeowners there are they're like, "Oh yeah, I bought my home through the CLT and, wait, everybody did this!" They have an idea of the power they have because there's now so many of them. I don't think a lot of them understood that they weren't just some random, lucky person that just got a house. They begin to see that we are really building a bigger community. And they get excited about that.

But I don't know if they really understand the organizing piece, at least not the way that we might understand the organizing piece as people who've been in organizing and have been advocating for affordable housing for awhile. I don't think they see it in that way. But when good things start to happen in their community, that is when they say, "Oh well, the CLT can help and we can go together and we can advocate."

The first homes that were in the CLT were built by the City of Houston. And the contractors that were used were not the best contractors. The CLT homeowners were frustrated. There were issues with their homes, so the homeowners called us. They were like, "I called the builder. I called the warranty company. I called the insurance company. Nobody could help me."

We advocated on their behalf and said, "We've got to get this fixed. This is not fair. You can't put people in houses like this." Then the homeowners were like, "I'm so glad y'all came. I'm so glad you were there to support me. I'm appreciative of you all being here to come and help."

When we then asked them, "Would you be willing to speak about your experience to help force the hand of these builders to do the right thing or to get the City to rectify the issue?" they step up and say, "Well, this is what I can do. I'll go to City Council and speak about this. I'll write a letter to support the Houston CLT. You want me to do an interview? Who do I need to talk to? I'll be more than willing to say what's going on."

They don't even realize they're doing advocacy. They don't even realize they're doing organizing by saying, "What do we need to do? Who do we need to talk to?" It just naturally happens. Whatever the issues that may come up they say, "Alright, let's go to the City and let's talk to the Mayor and let's get on the radio." It just naturally happens. They see us advocating for them, saying this is unacceptable, and we've got to do something about it. And they say, "Well, how can I help?"

Who is your "community"?

JOHN EMMEUS DAVIS: In a lot of the literature about community organizing and community development—even in a lot of conversations about community land trusts—people talk as if there's *one* community, as if everybody residing in a particular geography has the same set of material, political, and social interests. But in my experience, that's not an accurate picture of reality. I would assume in your neighborhood there must also be various interests, various divisions. Not everybody thinks that the land trust is the best deal in town. How do you, as a community-based organization, deal with some of those divisions?

ASHLEY ALLEN: Well, first, we're a city-wide land trust, so we absolutely have different interests and expectations and ways in which we support people. Geographically, within the city of Houston, people living in different places have different needs. And we're mindful of that.

We have what's called the "complete communities" where the Mayor has decided to focus for development and redevelopment. We are looking at their plans and thinking about how these particular neighborhoods are going to be changed and where we fit in with that.

We definitely take an approach of saying, "Okay, here are some areas where we know people are moving. Our buyers get to choose where they want to live." So that provides a data point. It lets us know what is the general community looking for in a home; where do they want to live; what kind of houses do they need?

The main divide is in communities that are gentrifying, between those who can ride out gentrification and those who could not. What we have to do is understand where the tension is and where the division is. We're really focused on those who need our help. Like, I'm a third-generation resident of this community, and I want to stay here. Or my grandmother stayed, but I had to move out because there were no apartments or houses that I could afford. Now I'm moving back because I want to be closer to my family. They are our priority.

JOHN EMMEUS DAVIS: So your priority is low-income and moderate-income households who are prospective homebuyers?

ASHLEY ALLEN: Correct. And those who are maybe not even prospective homebuyers, but they'll have no choice because their rent is so high. We've had several people come in and just say, "Well, at this point, I don't have any other choice. I can't afford my rent. My rent went up from $900 to $1,200. It ruined me, but there's no other place for me to go because everybody's rent is $1,200 now."

So they were now thinking about buying. They're starting to think about it differently. "Let me find a place where I can at least feel comfortable, where there's enough space for me and my family. Oh, I can also build some equity. Hmmmm. I can start putting something into savings."

So they're thinking about it differently. They weren't a prospective homebuyer. But the CLT showed them here's an opportunity that's going to save me from possible homelessness, because I can't afford to stay in my rental.

JOHN EMMEUS DAVIS: You're now working in multiple neighborhoods around Houston. Do you change your approach, change your message, change your organizing depending on which neighborhood you're entering?

Ashley Allen: Yes. The general message, of course, is still affordability, having a safe, affordable place to live. Because ultimately, for everybody that comes to us, their number one priority is affordability. It's not, "I want to invest because this is going to be my primary source of wealth for retirement." It's, "I need affordability now for me and my family. I need stability for me and my family." So that's why most people come to us.

The difference is who we reach out to in each neighborhood. Who are the trusted organizations in that community? Where are the trusted spaces?

In our first neighborhood, where we started getting homes, there was a multi-service center, a place that people would go to get help or information. We knew if we dropped our flyers in the multi-service center, we'd get a lot of people. The library was on a major intersection. So we would hold our events there because it was a respected place in the community. It was also right across the street from where our houses were being built. You could look out from the library and see there's a CLT home right there. It didn't seem like this abstract thing we were talking about. They could see we were telling the truth and there actually were homes coming.

But then you go to another neighborhood that might not have a multi-service center. So let's partner with another organization and get hosted at their offices because it's a respected space in the community. How we do our outreach does change, because there are different stakeholders in each neighborhood that are respected and are able to connect to that community.

I don't ever want to go in and just assume that I know how to connect with people, because I may not. We have to be mindful of that and understand that you just can't make one size fit all, especially in a place like Houston that is so diverse. You have communities like the Third Ward that have mansions and have shotgun houses at the same time. How do you engage both? Because you want the support of the people with the mansions, even as your priority is those who want to stay in the community but can't afford to.

Bridging racial, ethnic, and lingusitic divides

JOHN EMMEUS DAVIS: Houston is a city, like most cities in the United States, that is not only divided economically, but also divided racially, ethnically, linguistically. As you go into different neighborhoods, how does that factor into your organizing and outreach and message?

ASHLEY ALLEN: For us, our predominant languages are English and Spanish. So all our documents are in both languages. We're able to make sure that, when we're targeting particular neighborhoods where those are the top two languages. Our documents are in those languages. But we've recently added a translation service, so that if an instance comes up where somebody does speak another language, we have a way to make sure that we're supporting them.

That may especially be needed as we're expanding into other neighborhoods where other languages may be common. We want to make sure that we're thinking about what barriers could happen, no matter what neighborhood we work in. For some neighborhoods we know for sure it's going to be a language barrier. Or we know that there's going to be a technology divide, so we have to be conscious of those things.

It's not easy. I don't think we've perfected it by any means. But I think, as we're expanding into different neighborhoods, we're more conscious about how we can better support the different neighborhoods we're going into as we're expanding. Over time, the more experiences we have, the better we'll be able to create more policies and procedures to address the differences in the needs of every community.

JOHN EMMEUS DAVIS: How important has it been, given the diversity of the communities in which you work across the city, that you have built an organization where your staff and your board are people of color? The leadership of the Houston CLT is mostly

African-American. How important has that been in building relationships with people living in the neighborhoods you serve?

ASHLEY ALLEN: I think it's very important. There's the CLT idea of not owning land. I think it matters to have a person of color going in and explaining the land trust model because of the history of land being taken away from people of color. It was a very important connection for us being able to explain the history of the CLT and that it came from the Civil Rights Movement and what that means and highlighting that. Somebody who is White wouldn't completely ignore that, but it's very different for a person of color to highlight that history of the CLT model and to say where it came from and the significance of that.

JOHN EMMEUS DAVIS: This is a model that grew out of the African-American struggle in the South. People of color can claim it as their own. "This is ours. We invented it."

ASHLEY ALLEN: That part might have been missed—or the significance of that might've been missed—without a leadership that people in the community could relate to. When it comes to our board, yes, all of it is Black or Hispanic. I do think that's important.

Understand that, here in Houston, the homeownership gap for the Black and Hispanic community, compared to the White population, is very high. So making it a very clear priority for us to be able to create homeownership for those two populations is very important, creating strategies that make sense for those populations and communities.

I think it helps to have people who understand those communities and their unique perspectives and unique needs, having that relationship and building that trust. I think we benefit from having leadership of color. It's made it a lot easier for us to go into a neighborhood. We can understand and relate to what's currently going on in the neighborhood and what people are trying to protect and preserve.

Most CLTs are not run by people of color, of course. They work and they're successful. But here in Houston, because of what land means in Texas, I think it was very important for people to hear a person of color explain that it's not about giving up your land, but about the kind of collectivism that is common in cultures of color.

Becoming a part of "something bigger than yourself"

JOHN EMMEUS DAVIS: You've talked about working in multiple neighborhoods with multiple populations. What are the principal obstacles that you've faced? What would you say are the main barriers to getting people who are in your homes and residents who are in the surrounding neighborhood involved with your CLT?

ASHLEY ALLEN: Just getting people to understand the CLT model. It's not the easiest thing for people to grasp. I mean, the overall concept is pretty simple, but there are many complexities in the transactions and things. I think that's number one. And understanding that you're not just another nonprofit or just another housing organization, because of the collective ownership and the community aspect of the CLT.

We are getting ready to start building our organizational membership this year. We will have people from all over Houston helping to create the direction of the CLT, so we will be figuring that out. How do we get people to be members of the CLT, to want them to be involved, and to understand their role? Even if you're not a CLT homeowner, you still have a vested interest in the community; you still care about affordable housing and housing development and about not driving people out of the community.

I think one of the obstacles of the CLT model is getting people who can afford, you know, a $400,000 house to understand why it impacts them, why it matters that there's affordable housing in their community. I think that's a big one, having people understand the bigger implications of driving up home prices and displacing people.

Those are going to be our two biggest challenges: helping people to understand the CLT model and getting people to care about gentrification and the displacement of people in their community. Do you understand why the CLT is important? It can help prevent some of that from happening.

JOHN EMMEUS DAVIS: So this year you will be building a formal membership for the Houston CLT, even though you've had active resident involvement on the board?

ASHLEY ALLEN: Yes, and we've had residents going to City Council and saying why our program was important. They've already been doing those activities. But how do we formalize that, so our residents and also community members have a stake in the success of the HCLT.

JOHN EMMEUS DAVIS: Last October, when we organized the first World CLT Day, residents and staff of the Houston CLT were among the most actively involved in celebrating World CLT Day. There was energy. There was enthusiasm. It seems to me that, in your outreach to residents, you try to involve them not only in governance, but also in the more celebratory, social aspects of community building. Am I correct?

ASHLEY ALLEN: Absolutely. I think you create community through social interaction. We're celebrating together. We're seeing each other. We're seeing each other's families. It's like during our holiday event, where people are bringing their kids and their parents. It creates that sense of community, even if we don't all live together in the same neighborhood. Right now, we have homeowners in seventeen different neighborhoods and on opposite sides of town. They don't live anywhere near each other, but when we all come together, it feels like we are just one big community.

With World CLT Day, it wasn't just homeowners and staff. It was our board. It was some of our lenders and people from the title company. It was everybody who's been involved in our organization and who are part of the team that helps get somebody into a home. That was really an example of creating a larger community. It's not just the homeowners, but everybody who has a stake in seeing the success of the CLT.

Then in the summer we're having a picnic and everybody's having a good time playing games. And at the holiday party, we're passing out gift cards and having a good time. So it doesn't always have to be about the hard part in the advocacy and the fighting part. There's also that happy sense of being a community and just feeling good about being part of something bigger than yourself.

Being an organizer versus being a developer

JOHN EMMEUS DAVIS: Let's talk about the tension that exists in every CLT between being a community organizer, community builder on the one hand, and being a housing developer on the other. It's hard wearing two hats, being both an organizer and a developer. I'm wondering how you manage that tension inside your organization.

ASHLEY ALLEN: Well, we don't have that tension directly because we don't do our own development. Where the tension comes in is when we rely on other people to do the development and it's not done to the same standard that we would like. Then we become semi-developers and contractors. We start going out and looking at timelines to say, "Okay, at this point we should be 60% done. Why are we only at the foundation?" Or we're coming in and saying, "Hey, these bedrooms don't meet the standard size; this isn't going to work."

It's about making the homeowner our first priority. We have a stewardship responsibility. We're not just building housing and washing our hands. We have a different perspective than a traditional builder. We have a different perspective than maybe a municipality who's building affordable housing and selling it and then good luck trying to find somebody at local government to respond if there are any problems.

JOHN EMMEUS DAVIS: Connie Chavez at the Sawmill CLT in Albuquerque used to say, "We are the developer that doesn't go away."

ASHLEY ALLEN: Yes, exactly. You don't ever want to build something that's going to cause more problems later, because you're going to have to be the one to answer to that homeowner.

So for us, even if we were to become the developer, you want to be able to stand on what you advertise, to stand on what you promised. Like that quote, you have to be the developer that doesn't go away. For CLTs in particular, I think that makes you create higher expectations. You can't just lift your hands and walk away and say, "Oh, the warranty's up, so good luck." We don't have the luxury to do that. You have to be more mindful and put the buyer and homeowner as a top priority. You'll have to deal with it on the backend anyway. It's best to do it upfront to prevent longer issues later.

JOHN EMMEUS DAVIS: You're also accountable to the larger community at the same time that you're accountable to the CLT's homeowners.

ASHLEY ALLEN: Right. You don't want to be the bad neighbor. You know what I mean? Like just throwing up homes and then it's like, "Oh, they're driving down our property values." That's one of the things that we always talk about too. We don't want people being concerned about having affordable housing in their neighborhood.

What helps is that we also acquire existing homes that are currently on the market and make them affordable. It's the same house, but now it's more affordable; more people are able to live in it because the pool is now open to more than just those people who could afford a market price. We eliminate tensions when we don't build new houses that are affordable. We make houses affordable that are already there.

JOHN EMMEUS DAVIS: How about tensions among competing

city agencies? You're dealing with the Mayor's office. You're dealing with the land bank. You're dealing with the City's housing department. How do you navigate those cross-pressures?

ASHLEY ALLEN: We're not the one doing development, so we have a lot less of that. We're just a tool for people to use that helps them. Some of the housing organizations that we're closest to right now, when we first came on the scene, were very, very standoffish. They were like, "Oh, just another agency to take money. They're the new shiny thing and all the money is going to go to them." Once we explained to them how the model works and just kept building relationships, they were like, "Wait a minute, you all are going to be the best partner we have because you are coming in and making what we're building affordable. So now instead of serving 120% of AMI as our cap, we now can get all the way down to 50% or 60% AMI and help even more people. The CLT is going to come in and take what we have built and make it truly affordable." Once people understood the model and learned how they were going to get better results by using the CLT, they were more open.

Even with the City, we're giving them more numbers in single-family homeownership. It has been a challenge for them to get the numbers they're looking for, as far as helping people get into single-family homes. But through our program we're able to get them into homes pretty quickly. So now the City benefits from saying, "Hey, through our funding, the CLT has been able to get *x* number of people into single-family homes." And the City is using those numbers to be able to show results and to show where their money's going.

A lot of the nonprofit builders like Habitat for Humanity got hit really hard during the pandemic, because the price of lumber went up and labor was short. They're trying to build at affordable prices, but can't do it because of the conditions. So they started saying, "Our new target is more workforce housing, not low-income households. But here's the CLT and, with them, we can actually do what we want to do, helping people with a wider range of income."

It was just a matter of getting people to sit down and talk about what that partnership could look like. And them knowing that we're not competing; we're actually complementing each other, with benefits for both sides.

What keeps you going?
How do you keep your eyes on the prize?

JOHN EMMEUS DAVIS: We began today's conversation with a personal question about your earliest experience as a community organizer in Chicago. I think we should end by exploring another personal question: how to keep alive the values that drew you into this work originally. This is something that many mission-driven practitioners struggle with, especially those of us in the widening world of community land trusts.

In your personal life and in your professional career, you've come a long way from those homeless shelters you started in. You've earned an MPA and a PhD. You're now leading a highly successful nonprofit organization in the fourth largest city in the United States.

I have a sense, however, that you are still motivated by some of the same values and commitments to social justice that first brought you to community organizing. So my question to you is: How do you keep your eyes on the prize? Amidst the day-to-day demands of funding and administering the Houston Community Land Trust, how do you keep the faith? You've got people who are opposing the CLT. You've got city bureaucrats who are imposing requirements and restrictions that can make it difficult to do your work. How do you keep hope alive?

ASHLEY ALLEN: Oh, it's hard. It's difficult some days. In my first career, I was a scientist. I was creating food products. Sometimes you're just like, "Being in science is so much easier." Putting food products on the market is much easier than trying to solve major social ills, you know?

But ultimately, what keeps me going is what got me here, which was understanding and having empathy for the experience of those I'm trying to help. You never forget what it's like to see an eviction notice on the door. You never forget having to pack up your stuff in the middle of the night and have to get out. You never forget sleeping on the floor. You never forget eating in the cafeteria of the shelter. And the food sometimes has mold on it because it's old. You just never forget those things, even if you want to. Even with a lot of therapy, those memories are still there, still significant.

You never forget when you see a family that's coming to you and they're saying, "We gotta be out in sixty days. My landlord is selling the place because they're going to demolish it and put an expensive condo on it." You never forget what that feels like.

And that's what brought me into this space in the first place. That's what brought me into social services and nonprofit work in the first place. And that is what keeps me fighting. There are people who are depending on me. There are people who are depending on the City of Houston, people who are depending on our partners like the land bank, people who are depending on housing organizations and foundations to get them to a place of comfort, to get them out of their situation. And that keeps me going every day.

JOHN EMMEUS DAVIS: Do you ever get discouraged or ground down by all the meetings and all the minutiae of being an administrator and a supervisor and a fundraiser?

ASHLEY ALLEN: Yes. In the meetings I do, I'm sometimes speaking to people who don't know what it's like. You're speaking to a lot of people who, this is just a job for them. This is just a paycheck. But this is my value system. This is who I am as a human being. This is who I am every day. This is what I'm passionate about. Whether I'm getting paid for it or not, this is who I am. It's more than a paycheck to me, more than just a job to me.

JOHN EMMEUS DAVIS: It's a calling.

ASHLEY ALLEN: Yes. So when I'm going into these meetings and I'm getting bogged down, I do get angry if nobody is understanding what people are truly going through, if they're not putting people first. It is a challenge and sometimes you do get discouraged and some days I am like, "Okay, I'm done."

And then I remember that, again, there are people who are counting on me and my team and my board. It's the same way I was counting on somebody that, you know, helped me get into college. Or somebody who let my mom get into the shelter, even though she didn't meet the criteria, or somebody I was hoping would give me a job so I could support my family.

There were always people I depended on to get me to where I am today. So, if I can be that for somebody else, then I just have to keep on fighting. It's not easy. It's not easy at all, and I do get discouraged. But I just can't imagine allowing people to go through what I went through, if there's something I can do about it.

I'm not saying I'm the end-all-be-all. But if I can do even just a little bit to help somebody's situation, why wouldn't I do it? Because I know that I've benefited from other people's work and effort, sweat, tears, and donations. It's what I feel like I was born to do. My obligation is to give back.

JOHN EMMEUS DAVIS: Before we end, let me ask if there is any aspect of your work that we've overlooked in this conversation that you want to mention?

ASHLEY ALLEN: The only thing I would add is that I hope that the CLT movement continues. I think that it's definitely spreading. The conversations that I have weekly with different cities across the country let me know that people are thinking outside the box and moving away from traditional ways in which we have tried to provide affordable housing.

I think that's so important. Every day, there are more reports and stories about the housing market and how people are being priced out, how expensive things are getting for families. I get worried and concerned. How much worse can it get? How many people are going to end up unhoused because we've let the market get so out of control?

I just hope that, in the midst of all the craziness that's happening with the housing market, more people understand that we can start thinking about different ways to create housing affordability. It doesn't have to be the same old downpayment assistance. It doesn't have to be the same old homebuyer education. We can think of innovative models—with the CLT being one of them—and making them grow in places that are really, really hurting right now. Houston included.

JOHN EMMEUS DAVIS: I believe that a lot of people are benefiting from what you and the Houston CLT are doing for them. And a lot of people, here and abroad, are going to be both informed and inspired by what you've had to say today. I appreciate you taking the time to have this conversation. It's been a total pleasure. Thank you.

8.

Concluding Thoughts: Community Land Trusts as Scaffolding for Continually Thriving Communities

Theresa Williamson
July 25, 2022

[Editor's note: The panel discussion that begins this book was moderated by Theresa Williamson. It ends with a meditation by the same reflective practitioner, who was asked to discern common threads of aspiration and action running through the preceding chapters, viewed through the lens of her own experience supporting resident engagement in favela communities in Rio de Janeiro.]

So much that we value and take for granted in our cities is as it is thanks to the efforts of those who came before us acting, advocating, or organizing for it to be so. Some even lost their lives to make those changes happen, or to inspire those changes. Look around you and think of the qualities of the neighborhood where you currently sit, qualities that you most appreciate. Chances are someone fought for them, or better, a group of people fought for them. These were people with a common purpose or a shared geography—*a community*—that derived its satisfaction not from being remembered but from being part of the process that made that change happen, a hoped-for legacy that would be left for others, even if they themselves didn't live to see it materialize.

Throughout *Community Matters*, the critical role of community organizers and the importance of community—the "C" in CLT—are spotlighted by each practitioner, despite the dramatically different scenarios, needs, opportunities, contexts, and cultures that each community land trust is responding to. Each practitioner spoke to a local reality, reminding us that just as community matters, context matters! Yet a number of commonalities, particularly around the role of community and organizing, can be discerned.

The multigenerational, ongoing role of organizing was highlighted throughout the book, as were CLTs as a high-potential, effective scaffolding supportive of that continuous evolution. Though they're touted as a solution for affordable housing, the book's practitioners make clear that CLTs are about much more than building homes. As Dave Smith explains, "That's what other developers do: they come and build a building and then they go away because it's ended. But we're...in the business of building homes and *continually thriving communities*."

Addressing the gamut of human needs

The best community land trusts thus strive to be engines of community-building, working to meet the gamut of human needs at a scale where people thrive. This starts with *shelter*, yes. But today we know housing to be a necessary precondition to achieving the *security* necessary for individuals to access many other rights and opportunities. From a sense of security and safety, people are able to invest emotionally and connect with others, from which the need for *belonging* and *connection* is met. In turn, working together, residents can focus on other needs, from basic needs like food, as Dudley Street's gardens exemplify, to *self-actualization*, as the Caño CLT's Leadership Academy promotes in San Juan. CLTs also provide a secure base from which to achieve financial security and to raise a family, as Tony Hernandez describes. And within which migrants can find a new sense of belonging, as is taking place in Brussels.

At a minimum, CLTs are working to provide, as Ashley Allen explains, "a place to be *stable*, to not get kicked out, to be able to afford to stay put, both today and tomorrow." But stability is the foundation of so much more. Even those of us marked by privilege have gained an appreciation for this in light of the pandemic and climate crises.

In Rio de Janeiro, I have the honor of being a part of the Favela-CLT Project which has recently advocated for CLTs in municipal legislation. In coming years, we hope to have a pilot community land trust, inspired by the Caño CLT in Puerto Rico, that would be organized in one (or more) of our informal settlements. Stability is a key to why we are fighting for CLTs. Here, CLTs are also about preserving values that residents have built into their historic favela communities. CLTs are about creating the means for existing communities to stay and to maintain their already deeply-met need for belonging. As was done in Dudley Street, as is happening in Houston, and as was emphasized in San Juan.

Trust, engagement and power

This isn't easy. As Alejandro Cotté Morales puts it, our hegemonic, capitalist system is "always looking for ways to . . . undermine the collective. So part of the support to be given by organizers is to constantly *open up spaces for critical thinking and community organization*."

María E. Hernández explains how the logic shifts when organizers work to build a common understanding of community: In the

Caño, "before the community land trust was created, people said they were *divided* by the canal. But now, they are *united* by the canal. They have a vision now, just one vision for the community."

How did the Caño CLT open up spaces for critical thinking and unite residents like this? There was a shift in worldview from the logic of individualism to that of community. From the starting point of community, all needs can be met.

Another recurring theme across the practitioner stories in *Community Matters* is the critical nature of developing *trusted relationships* that in turn produce *engagement* and, ultimately, *power*. Such relationships can only be built through a long-term commitment, which is a characteristic of CLT practitioners.

Alejandro Cotté Morales makes clear that the primary engagement to be nurtured in a CLT is with those living closest, or who are most impacted, by the topic of interest. By focusing first and foremost on those at the center—residents—trust can be built. But trust-building exercises are still needed, as Razia Khanom has indicated, if residents who are part of marginalized or traumatized communities are to be engaged in a CLT's activities.

An important part of effective CLTs' trust-building is their commitment to being representative and reflective of the communities they serve. As Ashley Allen describes the experience of her own CLT in Houston:

It's very different for a person of color to highlight the history of the CLT model and to say where it came from and the significance of that.... Having leadership of color [has] made it a lot easier for us to go into a neighborhood. We can understand and relate to what's currently going on in the neighborhood and what people are trying to protect and preserve.... I think it was very important for people to hear a person of color explain that it's not about giving up your land, but about the kind of collectivism that is common in cultures of color (Chapter Seven).

Another ingredient in building trust is the set of interpersonal relationships that result from engagement and that can produce action. By engaging residents, often in a lighthearted and familial way as with Dudley Street's cookouts, residents are ready when action is needed. This is without having to be full-time organizers themselves. Tony Hernandez expresses it well in Chapter Three when he says, "Constant relationship building...is what's going to build trust; and that's what's ultimately going to build power." He describes how these relationships are formed:

> I don't want to run into Jason once a month for a check-in. But I do want to wish him a Merry Christmas.... 'What's going on in your life? What's new and exciting?' Let's build the relationship so that it doesn't feel like business every time we have an encounter. It feels like we're one big family. On occasion, yes, family business has to be handled. But on other occasions? Let's just be family. Let's have a cookout.

Ashley Allen says it's in community engagement and stewardship that the Houston CLT is currently investing, "because the best organizers...are happy homeowners." Consequently, if their CLT needs to organize, they "have an army ready."

Tony Hernandez summarizes in this way; he says that with the "triple E's"—engagement, education and empowerment—"the rest should fall into place." Echoing Ashley, he says that if collective action is later needed (such as when administrations change) the community can resume the fight.

All of the practitioners in the present book make clear, however, that fighting shouldn't be a constant in the process of building and sustaining a CLT. Every case cited a relationship to public authorities, whether passing a law (Brussels and San Juan), winning the respect of city officials (Houston), achieving eminent domain (Boston), or harnessing municipal resources (London and Houston). The fight is framed as part and parcel of achieving those victories, but the primary focus should always be on resident engagement and responsiveness, investing in the virtuous process of community-building that produces a reservoir of power that can be drawn upon and applied when needed.

From grassroots to meta community-building: a virtuous, sustainable cycle

Though focused on addressing the basic need for housing locally, these practitioners are all working to build much more than housing and something much bigger than their local CLT. CLTs operate in *layers* of community. There are the residents, allies, and advocates within a neighborhood and across a city—and their partners. But there are also layers of community and CLTs across their nation and across the world. Because of the cooperative nature of CLTs, we naturally form a broader ecosystem of mutual support.

Mutual support starts within the CLT, as exemplified by Tony Hernandez's summary of his basic role: "How do we serve as a resource, and help [CLT homeowners] take advantage of being in the land trust? How do we educate and empower the people to be able to carry this forward and to help the CLT to grow?"

Ashley Allen and various contributors speak of the immediate community around their CLTs: "Even if you're not a CLT homeowner, you still have a vested interest in the community; you still care about affordable housing and housing development and about not driving people out of the community."

Then there are the outer layers of that community. Razia Khanom described this after participating in an online event with our Brazilian CLT movement: "That is also part of my community now. It's a movement that we've all started. Attending that discussion with Brazil left me feeling renewed in my energies. That's what we do in communities. We help each other. We support each other. And we're also inspiring each other."

Here in Rio de Janeiro, we saw this in the pre-Olympics period when communities were targeted with forced eviction and 80,000 lost their homes, even people in favelas who had land titles. This is what led us to look at CLTs. They had the potential of being a more empowering solution, as opposed to individual titles that promote a divisive, atomizing, and exploitative logic.

During this period, community organizers in the favela most famous for its resistance efforts, *Vila Autódromo* (which is today among those interested in piloting a CLT in Brazil), would speak of allies as critical to their resistance efforts, for providing the energy and inspiration that helped them maintain their commitment to resist what felt like overwhelming pressure, as they were left living amidst the debris of forced evictions all around them.

Yet their allies felt the same: *Vila Autódromo's* organizers inspired us to keep fighting alongside them. Their determination and "not everyone has a price" mindset was palpable and gave us a sense of hope that all was not lost in this world. What was established was a virtuous cycle of mutual empowerment, inspiration and support. A determined local community inspired a broader community that was determined to support them, which in turn reinforced residents' conviction and commitment. The result: a self-sustaining system of mutual empowerment.

These meta communities, these ecosystems of civil society with mutually interdependent and supportive niches, these are community too! All with a broader collective and ultimate goal of realized human beings and a healthy, abundant planet.

Seven generations thinking

Community land trusts are complex. It is no accident that it has taken five decades for the model to begin obtaining global recognition. There's still a long road ahead. Highly-effective CLTs are not easy to set up, precisely because they're not just about physical structures: they are about building trusting relationships, collective decision-making, ongoing education, and taking the time to bring everyone along for the ride. And this is on top of the financial cost of acquiring access to land, constructing housing and other community elements, establishing supportive legal instruments and, perhaps most difficult of all, achieving the structural shift from an *individualistic* logic model to a *collective* one that a CLT requires and inspires.

It is a wonder so many CLTs have been created. At the same time, now that we know their transformative potential, it is paramount that the model gains massive traction. Dave Smith reflects:

> I don't think there's ever a business or a system where autocracy
> doesn't move things forward quicker. But you've got to ask
> yourselves about what it is, ultimately, that you value coming
> out the end of it. We could probably knock our houses up cheaper
> and quicker if we didn't involve people in the process.

But what if the equation takes into account all of the human needs that can ultimately be addressed through the scaffolding of a highly effective CLT? Does the cost-benefit ratio shift? Isn't it more efficient than a hodgepodge of on-again, off-again policies addressing one need at a time and then stumbling and unraveling one solution as we address another need?

What if we take a step back and view CLTs—and our world— through a sustainability lens? What if we apply seven generations thinking, a stewardship approach that suggests we live and work for the benefit of the next seven generations?

Our animal minds have trouble with long-game calculations. If our goal is quickly putting up lots of houses, then autocracy is king. But if our goal is self-actualized humans thriving in societies and on a healthy planet, where housing is but one of many interdependent needs that need to be met in reaching that goal, then a more robust scaffolding is needed.

Which brings us back to the CLT as a practical, beautifully-designed scaffolding tool to realize this potential. Ingredients of this scaffolding have been described or alluded to throughout this chapter, but there were also others mentioned in the previous chapters, such as the right to the city, asset-based community development (ABCD), nonviolent communication (NVC), and the productive role of conflict.

Ultimately, there is a simple, elegant, and more to-the-point way to describe this same possibility: the Reverend John Whitfield's vision for a "Be-love Community."

Sadly, the Reverend John passed away prior to the publication of *Community Matters*. Fortunately, we still have his opening meditation in Chapter One on "building the beloved community" where he made clear for us the direction in which he hoped the CLT movement is headed:

> I submit to you this morning that the CLT movement of the 21st Century and beyond must strive to take the beloved community to the next level and work towards creating and maintaining "Be-love Communities"...that...would not only simply represent bricks and mortar,...but would be a catalyst that will move this world toward a place of realizing that we must crucially come together in the spirit of unity...where individuals know without a shadow of a doubt that what they're doing is not simply a matter of providing housing with affordability in perpetuity. We're creating an atmosphere of love.

May we continue organizing, relating, and engaging together, bringing everyone into the fold, charging forward to realize the Reverend John Whitfield's inspiring vision.